TO DATE,
LIKE NORMAL

BY
BRIANA BILLER

Copyright © 2021 Briana Biller

Contents

ACKNOWLEDGEMENTS

Thank you to my unconditionally loving and supportive family. My moms, Rosemary and Susan, my sister, Dondra have been my unwavering support system through every battle and learning experience along this journey.

I am honored to thank Dr. Lorraine Platka-Bird and Dr. Leah Leonard for coaching me through, and over, seemingly insurmountable obstacles. Thank you to every single nurse and staff member at the Center for Hope of the Sierras, as well as the women I spent the summer with. Thank you for being my inspiration by simply just existing in your beautiful selves.

My best friends who keep me laughing and help me maintain an objective reality when I feel myself jumping onto the "crazy train." Thank you for providing me perspective and a place to exist safely in my emotions.

And thank you for picking up this book, having faith in yourself, and the courage to examine your own life in the process.

TO DATE, LIKE NORMAL

My story is shared by millions. Our story goes wildly misunderstood. There is no shame in my story.

Several years ago, I trudged through the doors of a residential treatment facility, close to death. If not physically, I was emotionally dead. My eating disorder was killing me and I had surrendered.

For fourteen years I'd been trapped by a tyrannical eating disorder that controlled everything I did and every decision I made. Every second of my life was controlled by a voice in my head that said I'd never be good enough, never be thin enough. It convinced me that I was worthless and needed to be punished. I needed to be perfect. I never did anything right. The more I tried to appease the voice in my head, the louder and more powerful it got. That was the power of my eating disorder.

While in treatment, I worked to untangle this mess and find my own identity separate from that of the eating disorder. To this day, I'm still in the process of discovering who I am and learning to live my life free of this disorder. I've spent years making recovery-oriented decisions, making choices I know are right- even when my eating disorder is screaming at me. I've taken the time to develop relationships the eating disorder would never have let me. I've spent the last 10 years creating a life that I want to live.

I am alive- exactly the opposite of what the eating disorder wanted me to be. I look back on who I used to be, the girl struggling within an inch of her life, and it feels like a separate identity, a dark past-life. I am blessed I have come this far. I worked really hard and accomplished things I never knew I was capable of. Even a year after discharge, I was buzzing with life and an energy I never knew existed. I was able to return to the treatment facility to talk to the residents there about my recovery process. I've been able to return several times to share my recovery experience.

I chose to write a book and share my story because struggling with, and recovering from an eating disorder is gruesome. The process was emotionally violent and hideous. I didn't understand what I was going

1

through and my experiences perplexed everyone around me. It was an experience worse than anything I could have imagined in my worst nightmare. As I tried to break free, the eating disorder endlessly told me that I would never accomplish my goals while not in its company. It made me believe that I was flawed, and worthless, while not in its grips.

I had to live through unbearable discomfort. I had to be fearless and courageous. Now that I am successfully in recovery, I know it was worth every second.

This narrative is my experience. There are no facts, research, or scientific studies to support any statements in this book. It is one person's experience. It is my experience with a life-threatening disorder. It is my process- my successes and failures. I know many can relate. I know many have experienced similar and unique struggles of their own. Read this book, let it guide you in developing your own process. Share this book with your support system, so they can get a glimpse inside the experiences you are going through.

While I was suffering, I wanted to believe that I was the only one who knew how to have an eating disorder. I thought I was the only one doing it right. I knew the rules. I knew my eating disorder inside and out, and no one else could participate. I know this is not the case. I now understand that many others are suffering, using their eating disorder as a form of identity. Everyone has their own rules and special, very intimate, relationship with their eating disorder. I am not the only one who struggles. And neither are you.

Part of my recovery is accepting that I am not perfect. This book is not perfect. It is user-friendly and easy to read. And while it may be hard to digest at times, it is honest and practical. It is a means to gain insight; for those struggling as well as their support systems. I provide valuable insight for friends, family, significant others on what the struggle is like, and how one woman overcame obstacles regarding her own eating disorder.

To anyone observing an eating disorder, to those not directly in its grips, eating disorders are completely illogical. The impulses and behaviors leave our support systems clueless on how to help. This book will provide some insight into the logic of eating disorders and provide some understanding for the ever-loving support systems.

If you've picked up this book, you're probably familiar with the concepts of Anorexia and Bulimia and their related behaviors, but if you're just beginning to learn: those affected by anorexia refuse food due to an intense fear of weight gain and often perceive their bodies as larger than reality. They do not maintain a weight appropriate for their height, and their weight often falls below 85% of what is expected for their height. The final diagnostic criteria for women affected by anorexia is a loss of menstrual cycle for three consecutive months.

Many definitions of Anorexia include "loss of appetite", which is frequently misunderstood. In my experience, I was trying to control my appetite, trying to control my hunger. I was trying to deny that I had any appetite at all.

Professionals diagnose Anorexia Nervosa in two different categories. The first is characterized by restricting food intake to maintain a low body weight. The second is characterized by restricting as well as engaging in binge-purge behaviors to maintain a low body weight. Bingeing and purging consists of engaging in episodes of overeating followed by abuse of laxatives, over-exercising, fasting, and self-induced vomiting. Those affected by Anorexia Nervosa can be diagnosed in either of these two categories.

Bulimia Nervosa is diagnosed by engaging in two or more episodes or bingeing and purging in a week for more than three months. Those affected by Bulimia often maintain a weight normal for their height. Over a span of almost 15 years, I experienced Bulimia Nervosa and Anorexia Nervosa- bingeing purging type.

These strict, sterile, and cold criteria, do not acknowledge the mental struggle. I believe the proper diagnosis is irrelevant to recovery. I believe that any unhealthy relationship with food and/or weight, enough to interfere with daily life, needs to be treated just as seriously as those that match the criteria. Any unhealthy relationship with food, any disordered eating is a manifestation of a deeper mental crisis and should be taken very seriously. The mental battlefield makes this a very serious illness that frequently goes unaddressed.

In this book, I will refrain from identifying myself as "anorexic" or "bulimic". I will instead use the terms, "affected by anorexia and bulimia." This is because those of us affected often identify ourselves by our eating disorders. It quickly becomes one's entire identity. I want to discourage this behavior. By saying that I am an anorexic, or bulimic, it makes the eating disorder my identity. I am not an eating disorder. I have worked hard for years to separate myself out from my eating disorder and no longer identify myself based on these labels. I am affected by these mental disorders but they no longer make up my identity. I encourage you to do the same.

Eating disorders cannot be linked to a single cause. They are a *biopsychosocial* disorder, with roots biologically, socially, and psychologically. There are several factors that lead to the development of Anorexia Nervosa and Bulimia Nervosa, and it is never the same for two people. I've discovered, through my recovery process, that distorted body image, dysfunctional family dynamics, my intense desire for perfection, high anxiety and depression, with a longing to escape from my emotions led to the development of my eating disorder. I learned that my eating disorder led me to use my body to express what I did not know how to express emotionally.

I was blessed with an amazing treatment team who helped me discover all of these truths. My therapists, nutritionists, and psychiatrists helped me untangle all the aspects of the eating disorder. They helped me figure out why I developed it in the first place, so I could unwind myself from its talons. While in treatment, I uncovered many aspects of the eating disorder. I discovered it is a coping mechanism. I discovered why I needed it and how it served me in my life. I discovered that the behaviors are methods to handle the difficulties and problems that arise in my life.

This is the story of my recovery. From my struggle, to my time in treatment where I untangled my disorder, to my discharge, and even stages of advanced recovery- how I live my life now. This is the story of how one woman began to live her life without an eating disorder.

To those struggling, you deserve to have your daily battles acknowledged. You do not need to be accused of vanity, confusion, or 'going through a phase'. Your struggle is a very real one that not many will understand.

One of the most memorable, albeit discouraging, moments from early on in my attempts at recovery, occurred when I was deep in my suffering. I went to see a counselor on my college campus. I told her my symptoms: that I couldn't eat and everything I did eat, I threw up. I was begging for help. She told me to "keep a journal and drink less coffee." I walked out hopeless that I'd ever be normal; hopeless that I'd ever be able to sit at a table and share, much less enjoy, a romantic dinner with a significant other.

This debilitating disorder made even the most mundane, normal tasks of life seem impossible. Life events, such as going out with friends, dating, going to school, even holding a job, seemed unfeasible. I fight for my recovery because I want to feel normal, I want to do normal things that make up a healthy life.

I encourage you to find your own motivations for recovery and hold it close to your heart. I want to hold a job. I want to go to the beach. I want to go out with friends. I want to go shopping. I want to be able to go on a date. I want to laugh over dinner with someone I love, uninhibited, with my own personality- not that of my eating disorder. Someday, I want to be able to eat cake at my wedding. Find your motivation and let it carry you through your recovery process.

To those struggling, you deserve hope; there is life outside the eating disorder. I want to provide you with hope. I want to provide you with examples of how someone overcame seemingly insurmountable obstacles on the road to recovery. I want to acknowledge the internal war waged. I want your support system to get a glimpse of the daily battles, the relapses, and the desire to seem perfect in recovery. Eating disorders affect everyone in our surroundings, and they deserve hope too. Through all of the struggles, remember that recovery is possible.

I encourage you to read this book while seeing your therapist regularly. I recommend journaling, writing down everything that surfaces, recording every emotion and every step of your recovery. The first piece of recovery is being open and honest with yourself about what is occurring with you at any given moment. Stay mindful, pay attention. Everyone's eating disorder is different and unique. Your process will be different from mine. Let your recovery be unique to you. Let your recovery be a part of your new identity. Get emotional; angry, sad, and proud of your successes. Allow yourself to feel these emotions as they surface, as uncomfortable as they will be. Be open about your experience. The eating disorder has been a way for you to hide emotions and numb yourself from feeling anything. Allow yourself to start feeling emotions, acknowledge their presence in your life, and process through them.

Eating disorders are biopsychosocial disorders that need to be untangled in order to find their roots and discover a path to recovery. Remember that recovery is a process, with successes and failures, and you figure it out on the way.

Thank you for picking up this book, I hope it helps bring you to life.

I FORGIVE MYSELF, RELEASE THE PAST, AND MOVE FORWARD WITH LOVE IN MY HEART

My life as a pursuit of the ideal body

The development of my eating disorder can be illustrated as a life dedicated to the pursuit of the ideal body. When I was seven, I decided I wanted to be a model. I heard that models are skinny and focus on losing weight. When I expressed this desire to my mother she replied, "Just don't get too focused on it. You know, some women get so wrapped up in losing weight, they stick their fingers down their throats to make themselves throw up."

"Ew, Mom. Gross."

One of my friends was a model. She modeled for JC Penny and criticized my smile. She suggested we go on a fruits and veggies diet to lose weight. This started a 15 year war against my body that would dominate a childhood and disallow the development of a healthy life. This was the same year that my parents divorced and my body became my emotional punching bag. I needed a distraction from my emotions. I needed to focus on something other than my parents' separation. I focused on my body. I focused on my weight.

Growing up, I felt I was constantly overshadowed by my overachieving older sister. I was often in my own world, trying to make up my own successes and trying to seek acknowledgement. I was always making up goals to prove my self-worth. I could never keep up. My dad and sister were always ditching me, in conversations, out on adventures, and they were constantly leaving me behind. My legs wouldn't carry me fast enough to keep up on our hikes and my imagination wanted me to play along the way- it distracted me at every turn. I wanted to walk on logs, find animals in the clouds, and watch bugs. No one noticed that I was always several paces behind. I was never good enough, and I was never perfect. I began striving for unachievable goals in order to get attention. I always had a voice in my head that had me striving for perfection, always encouraging me, and always setting the bar just out of my reach.

I remember the morning of the jacket. I don't think my mother even remembers this episode, but it is still crystal clear to me. It was Winter and my mom had just bought my sister and I new jackets. I had never thought about how I looked in a jacket before. This one was a parka. Parkas were practical, worn in the snow (I grew up in the mountains and I knew this). But this particular morning, I had my jacket on early, eager to wear my new jacket to school and play in the snow. I was waiting to leave and caught a glimpse of myself in the mirror. I was horrified. The jacket made me look fat. I always thought I was pudgy, but this particular morning, I was so fat there was no way I was going to wear the jacket in public. No way I was going in public with this body. I felt so disgusted with myself, I took it off and refused to put it back on.

My self-loathing grew to an out-of-control rage with myself. I took this rage out on my mother as we engaged in a full-blown fight over wearing the coat. We fought until we were both crying. I was not going to wear that layer of fat. I hated myself. I hated my mother for trying to push that on me. In order to stay home from school, I claimed I was sick so I wouldn't have to face the world. My mother won the argument and I reluctantly wore the fat suit to school. My head was bowed down all day long because I was so depressed about how fat I was. Kids asked me what was wrong- it was obvious I had been crying. I explained that I was tired and wasn't feeling well.

It was the first day I can remember feeling fat all day long. I was seven years old.

I accepted then that I was fat. That I would look fat in everything, and that someday I would be skinny. Someday. I went through my childhood believing that I was different, feeling pity for anyone who had to look upon my body. I went through my childhood feeling insignificant compared to my peers, even though I was smart, talented, and dedicated. I hated the body I was trapped in and felt bad for anyone who was associated with me. I was embarrassed because I didn't think anyone should have to look at my body or tolerate being friends with the "fat girl". I thought my legs looked like baby seals, huge rolls of blubber. I stopped wearing shorts. I was always given the larger sized soccer uniforms. They were baggy on me, making me look even bigger. I'd cringe away from team photos. You couldn't see the tendons in the back of my knees, like you could on the "skinny girls" on my soccer team.

I had an 'outty' belly button. I thought it was because I was fat, that there was no room inside me for my belly button, that when I grew up and got skinny, my belly button would go in like everyone else's.

My awareness of my size encouraged me to try endless diets to fit in. As I grew up I discovered that dieting became a way to impress my mother. It became habit to contemplate the fat content of everything I put in my mouth. Whether it consumed my life as a child or not, the thoughts, and fears, of gaining weight were always there. I kept track of everything I ate compared to everyone else. I always ate a little bit less than everyone around me. I rationalized that if I could eat less, I'd be the thinnest. I found out my nickname behind my back at school was Big Bri. Everyone else knew I was fat too.

But I wasn't fat. Growing up, I was a normal, healthy sized child. I played soccer and did children's theatre. I took dance classes and engaged in many activities. I was athletically built. I developed faster than other girls my age. This led me to believe I was bigger, fatter. The way I perceived my body was severely distorted. This body image distortion began in my early childhood and continued well into my adulthood- I even grapple with it on a much smaller scale to this day.

The desire for the ideal body, to fit into the perfect image I had in my head, made me diet all through junior high. I became exhausted from erratic eating patterns. The carbohydrate-free diet left me lethargic. I would swell with pride when my friends asked me why I was so tired. I would reply confidently, "I'm on this new diet." I would find my confidence, and pride, in those words, "I can't, I'm on a diet." Dieting made me superior when I was actually depressed and self loathing, looking for an answer to my body hatred. But I always had the diets. I had the control. I had the power. Dieting gave me something that no one else had. I had weight loss goals. I had self control. I was going to be skinny. "Haha, suckers," I'd think.

I kept trying to follow my sister's lead and her desire for weight loss, as it seemed to impress our mother. I could diet better than my older sister, and I held that close to my heart. I was ready for any diet, in order to get the ideal body. I was trying to impress anyone I could glean attention from. I wanted everyone to notice when I didn't eat. I wanted them to notice my fitness, my strength, my will power.

I completely disregarded the respect my classmates and teachers had for me because I was a hard worker. They had respect for me because I was talented, friendly, loving, confident, and intelligent. I didn't believe any of it at the time; more importantly, I didn't care. I wanted everyone to think I was skinny and athletic. I wanted to look good in the trendy, colorful, Bubblegum Jeans. I wouldn't eat in front of anyone except my family.

When my mom would criticize my sister for 'eating mindlessly' (as she called it), the comments were fuel for me to not eat at all, or to flaunt how well I was dieting. 'Mindless Eating' was a term my family used with frequency, to indicate when someone was eating because they were bored or didn't have anything better to do. It means not thinking about your eating but 'eating mindlessly'. My mom was constantly worried that my sister was doing this to distract herself from the emotional pain of our parents' divorce. I even tattled on my sister once for having the 'mindless munchies', but really it had been me who'd eaten all the Eggos- I just didn't want to get punished for it.

My eating disorder didn't let me eat cake or pizza at birthday parties. It didn't let me eat anything more than fruits or veggies at lunch time. It made me take an entire lunch period to eat one corner of a quesadilla. I wanted to feel skinny. I wanted to appear thin and in control. I wanted people to think I was skinny. I wanted them to envy me and give me attention for my self discipline.

Mornings after slumber parties, I'd wake up famished and hate myself for being hungry when the other girls, the 'skinny girls' didn't ever seem hungry.

"No wonder I'm so fat. I'll never fit in. Life would be so much easier if I wasn't so hungry or chubby," I'd think to myself.

My quest for the ideal body, and the lifestyle I believed it would bring me, led me to judge every day and every episode of my life by how I felt in my clothes that day. If I could wear, and look skinny and sexy, in a certain top it was a Good Day. And *"good for me"*, I was allowed to have fun. That was hardly ever the case. More often were the days when I didn't look thin, didn't fit the ideal. I would hide away, depressed, anxious, hating myself, wondering if I would ever know what it was like to be thin.

Someday, I'd think, *someday, I'll know what it is like to be skinny.* And I kept pursuing the ideal body.

Through junior high school, I got perfect grades, in advanced classes. I never got detention. I received awards for perfect attendance. I received Golden Star Student awards. Our house was full of these certificates. They got filed away, a stack of my sister's and my perfect report cards and Honor Roll certificates. We never got rewarded for our grades, our parents expected nothing less of us. I set school records in track and field. I won talent show competitions. I placed well in cross-country running races. I was perfect.

One day, in eighth grade, at Track and Field practice, I wasn't pushing myself as hard as the coaches were accustomed. The track coach said, "What happened?"

I replied, rather jokingly, "I got fat." He looked me up and down, and laughed in what could only be interpreted as agreement. So apparently that's why I didn't set any more school records. That was my reasoning for anything not going my way. I got fat.

My high school years are marked by theater performances, dance recitals, and by my weight.

Going into high school, I felt that the constant dieting wasn't working. I still felt too chubby to be accepted. My sister and I went to the gym everyday after school. I'd had a gym membership since I was 10. We went tanning too. I was able to have fun with my friends, but in the back of my mind was the haunting reality that *someday* I needed to be skinny. I was just not there yet.

Becoming thin was a constant, haunting, unmet need. I was thinner than most of my friends, but I was not the thinnest. As long as I was not the skinniest, it didn't matter. I started cutting down on my food intake, little by little. In addition to dance classes, rehearsals for school plays, and going to the gym everyday, I would do endless amounts of situps and pushups, and stretches in my bedroom when I was not consumed with homework. I had a skinny dance teacher that year, and she put me in the back of the dance formations. I was full of self-loathing. I thought I was put in the back, because I was fat, that my body was not suitable for the front row. I got furious with myself for being fat. After dance class, I would go home and get in a scaldingly hot bathtub (the pain distracted me), wishing the heat would melt my fat away. And I would cry. I thought that not having the ideal body was discrediting my dance talent.

I began replacing my daily food intake with celery and chewing gum, both would allow me to deny my hunger- I can still smell the fruity gum that would keep me from eating. I had a special way to eat the celery. I would bite off one corner, and pull the strings off with my teeth. Once all the strings were gone, it left the tender inside of the celery stick. I would proceed to suck on this for hours. This would occupy much of my class time and a distraction from the desire to eat any other food.

Our dance team that year was given hideous, blue unitards for our performances at basketball games. People would comment that I was the only one on the team who looked good in them. These comments fueled my desire for more weight loss. I adored, craved, the attention I was getting for losing weight. I finally had flattery attached to my body and I desperately wanted more.

The first time I purged was on Super Bowl Sunday 2003. I had been restricting and over exercising severely for several months. My mom's partner made many snacks for the game. Creme puffs, spring rolls, mini quiches. These were snacks that my mother would usually never allow in the house. And I ATE. I ate so much, I thought I would explode. I ate so much I could barely crawl down the hall to my bedroom where I spent the next few hours painfully throwing up into my little purple trash can. I tried to stay quiet so my mother wouldn't hear. I was trying to redeem myself for everything I had just eaten, everything I had just ruined. I had to heave all that food out of me. I couldn't let it stay inside me. As painful as it was, being empty again was a relief I had never experienced. This was the first time I experienced purging.

Fingers down my throat, teeth slicing cuts on the back of my hand, trying to heave in silence. I didn't know I would spend the next thirteen years in a porcelain prayer.

"Ew, Mom. Gross."

I threw up every meal for months. It was such an easy answer. It was fun. I could eat anything, without worrying about it. Having worried about every single bite I'd ever put in my mouth, suddenly I had the answer. Eat anything, throw it up. No guilt. I would feel the pressure of food in my stomach and feel immediate relief after purging. I did this until my school's Winter Formal dance that year. The days leading up to the dance, I didn't eat. I loved my dress. We went to a seafood restaurant for dinner. It was easy for me to avoid eating because I'd been a vegetarian for years. I picked at a soup and salad, flattered and fueled by the comments I received, "That's all you're going to have? Are you sure?"

"I'm sure," I'd say, "I'm just too excited to be hungry."

I was proud of my restricting, proud of my emptiness, and I allowed myself to have fun and dance all night. The entire time I was dancing I was thinking about how many calories I was burning. I woke up the next morning and was going to throw up my breakfast, until I thought about how much fun I'd had the night before, and decided not to. Instead I tried to believe that I didn't have to beat myself up over my weight. And a boy finally had a crush on me. I'd had a crush on him for months; it felt good to have the attention returned.

At that point, I started to put weight back on. Those who've experienced eating disorders are familiar with the constant swing in weight. The roller coaster of weight gain, and loss, that comes along with erratic eating patterns; restricting and bingeing, hunger and fullness.

I chose to ignore the weight gain. I was still thinner than some of my friends, and I liked eating. I'd spent the majority of my childhood on a diet, eating was a new experience for me. I gave myself explosive freedom with food. I drank whole milk by the glassful and bread slathered in real butter. I binged on foods that I'd never let my lips touch in my entire life- foods that weren't allowed in our house.

I rationalized these bingeing behaviors with the notion that I'd always tried to be the "skinny" I so desperately wanted and it didn't work. I never got there. So I was doing the opposite. I'd eat what I want, binge but not purge. All the while I was 'revenge eating', in the back of my mind I knew that this was just a phase and, not to worry, someday I'd be skinny.

Everyone in high school was all shapes and sizes, I suddenly didn't feel like I stood out for being fat. My mom got me a whole new fat wardrobe. It consisted of all new clothes that fit me as I put on weight. That made me feel awful, embarrassed, like I was letting her down.

I was still dancing, but starting to worry that the costumes I'd ordered in October would not fit for recitals in the spring. I would purge, every now and then, without it helping me to lose weight. A month before recitals, I started to pick up on my parents' worries about my weight. They'd suggest I not drink so much milk. My mom would comment on how much I was eating and if I really *needed* all of it. I felt she was disappointed that I'd stopped trying to lose weight. Stopped pursuing the ideal body. She encouraged me to ask a doctor about it when I went for a routine physical. I knew I'd let her down. I knew she thought I was too fat again.

When I wasn't obsessing about it, my pursuit of the ideal body was looming on the horizon. Feeding myself was comforting. I started restricting again so I could fit into my dance costumes. They fit fine. They were tight. I didn't eat the weekend of the performances, and I attributed being able to fit into these costumes to not eating. I thought I looked heinous, once again. The material was stretched across my fat body and I was mortified.

I binged my way through that summer, wondering why my bike ride to work wasn't helping me lose weight. Hating my fat body again. Hating it and not knowing what to do about it. Again, my pursuit for the ideal body began, but in slow motion, taking on different forms.

My vegetarianism escalated to veganism. Being vegan was my excuse to not eat anything I deemed 'fattening'. It was my excuse to eat only soups, salads, and fruit bowls, nothing else. I did this for several months. I went with my sister to the gym, constantly in athletic competition with her. Tread-milling and sit-upping, we wouldn't let a day go by without going to the gym. I began to lose weight until I was at a steady weight, bingeing and purging every so often. I'd binge and purge when I felt like it. I'd purge when I felt I'd over eaten. I'd purge after eating in restaurants. But it wasn't habitual. It wasn't an addiction yet. And I wouldn't obsess or even think about it. I'd just throw up and be done with it.

Costumes were how I would gage my weight. Costumes that fit snug in November were loose by performances in the spring. Approval I got for losing weight, at this point, was tight knit with the approval I felt while receiving standing ovations in leading roles in school plays. And the approval continued when I went back to work that summer, more than 20lbs lighter than I was the year before. My coworkers took photos of how much weight I'd lost. I was getting tons of attention for looking cute and being smaller.

I would binge and purge regularly through the summer, but my weight would stay the same. The behavior was a good outlet and felt good. Sometimes I felt I couldn't control it, I just needed to binge and purge.

The following year, my junior year of high school, I was depressed and busy. I was able to claim that I didn't have time to eat. It was a perfect storm for my eating disorder. Between rehearsing for three shows and keeping up on my school work, I began losing weight. My addiction started to develop. It began to function for me. I was able to incorporate the behaviors into my daily life. The behaviors (bingeing, purging, and restricting) kept me away from anything outside of my eating disorder. My addiction dragged me through drive-thrus on the way home from rehearsals. It had me pre-planning binges through the days and during rehearsals. It made me short tempered with my family and not want to spend time with my friends. I hardly ever saw my mom anymore. I would wake up at 4:40 to be at the gym by 5 (the scale there was exactly three pounds off), to be at school by 6:45, where I would take my diet pills with coffee, and sit through classes while starving, my stomach aching, not focusing and not caring. My pursuit of the ideal body made me apathetic in my studies and on stage. In my free time, I binged and purged.

My pursuit of the ideal body made me isolate. It kept my head completely engrossed in one thing. I was a robot focused only on losing weight. Once I clicked into robot mode, it got easier. I became familiar with my behaviors and accepted them as normal. I became accustomed to abusing my body. I got used to the depression. I was familiar with having no energy, the pain was *just the way it was*. The thrill of dropping pounds was worth it to me.

In the Spring, my drama teacher had me swap costumes with a 'skinny girl' because my costume was much too big on me. I had lost enough weight to get the 'skinny girl's' costume. I barely remember performing in shows that year. All I remember was dancing to fit into that costume. I wanted to look the best. I wanted to be the best. I was going to be perfect. I was ticking off weight-loss goals everyday.

Because I was bingeing and purging so often, my mother would question me about the absence of large quantities of food from the house, and, in pursuit of the ideal body, I would deny everything. We had many fights. My pursuit of the ideal body made me lie to my mother, made me fight with her, made me explode in anger at her.

I purged so much, something in my throat stopped working. The muscle in my stomach that keeps food in, stopped working. To this day, my esophagus and the surrounding muscles do not work properly. If I eat a big meal and lean over forward, I physically have to tighten a muscle in my chest to keep my food in my stomach. At this point in my eating disorder, all I had to do was lean over. Eat, make sure I drank enough liquid, and lean over.

"Eew, Mom. Gross."

My mom found pieces of food in the drain of our shower, one of my frequent purge spots. She confronted me and made me go to Dr. Lorraine, my registered Dietician and Eating Disorder Specialist on May 9, 2005. I went along with the therapy, the treatment, proud of myself for "overcoming my eating disorder" and getting back in control of my behaviors.

It felt good for a while. It got my family off of my back, and I had permission to eat. For the first time in my life, I had permission to eat. I had earned the right to eat. I had starved and purged my way to unconditional permission to eat. And I ate. For a few months I didn't pursue the ideal body. I kept purging, not with the same frequency, but occasionally, without telling anyone, without telling my therapist.

My family was proud of me. My friends, who had been worried about me, were proud of me. For the time being, I let the pursuit of the ideal body go. In my mind, I got fat again. I knew that this was not the time in my life to get skinny. I just had to wait a little while. One day, *someday*, I would know what it was like to be skinny.

A few years went by and my body image did not improve. I moved around to a couple places in California. I went to school for a quarter at University California Santa Barbara. I'd go to the cafeteria on campus and binge. I'd use the bathroom in there to purge, and then binge again-all within the confines of the cafeteria. I'd then escape to my dorm and purge there. My roommates and I didn't get along. I didn't have any friends there, so no one was there to think this was abnormal behavior. I went to the dining hall once a day and went to the bathroom after my meal. Then I'd go get second helpings and visit the bathroom once again. I got away with a lot of eating disorder behaviors there, I'm glad I didn't stay very long.

I moved in with my sister in San Diego for a couple months. I continued bingeing and purging habitually, often several times a day. Not for weight management, but because it felt good. It was habitual and familiar to me.

I auditioned, got accepted, and enrolled in a two year performing arts academy called the Pacific Conservatory of the Performing Arts. My two years at PCPA were the most enlightening, magical, incredible years I could've ever asked for. I had always dreamed of attending a school where I was in theatre classes all day, every day. I had wanted it my whole life and I was finally there. I threw myself whole-heartedly into every class, every rehearsal, every party, every experience and gleaned a four-year education in the two years I was there. I made a family of 32 of the closest friends I ever had. I matured as a person, as an actor, and as an artist. I was able to do what I loved, every day for two years and learned everything I needed to go pursue the career I thought I always wanted.

Unfortunately the stress of being on such a hectic schedule and the amount of pressure I put on myself to get everything I could out of this school (and be perfect along the way), led me deeper into my eating disorder. The two years of amazing school, and relationships, is so entwined with my eating disorder, I can't imagine what it would've been like without it.

I arrived at school and was able to go two weeks without bingeing and purging. I desperately wanted my life at school to be free from my eating disorder and behaviors. I didn't want to taint my sacred world with my past demons. Then the night came where I had my first difficult homework assignments. While I was working, I ate through an entire box of granola bars- mindlessly snacking to appease the stress. I could feel my stomach protruding out over the top of my pants, the granola bars heavy and threatening. Terrified about the amount of weight I would gain, thinking of all the dance classes and auditions I wanted to look good for (in a school that was highly competitive), I reluctantly went to the bathroom and purged.

Free from the granola bars, free from the weight in my stomach- the relief spread through me and calmed me. It lulled me to sleep that night.

I binged and purged on a regular basis after that night, some days and weeks being worse than others. With the erratic schedule, I couldn't find a normal eating pattern and often found myself bingeing in the car on the way to rehearsals or classes. I'd purge wherever I could just to relieve stress before tasks. At that point, it was just a tool to relieve stress. A welcome distraction.

I went around hating my body, but thinking that it was not yet time to get skinny. I went on through this period using my disordered behaviors to manage stress, not to lose weight. I used it as a way to escape problems, to avoid issues. I always had the physical desire, need, to binge and purge, but I didn't believe it was consuming my life.

Every day, I'd wake up saying to myself, *"This is the day I will not indulge in my eating disorder."* And every night I'd go to bed hating myself because I somehow managed to engage in the behaviors anyway, regardless of the day's goal. My pursuit of the ideal body was waiting, hiding around the corner. I was not actively pursuing it, but I knew someday, *someday*, I'd be skinny.

I evaluated my body every day. I judged my days by how I looked, or fit, in certain outfits. The same battle I'd engaged in for years. I remember days by what I ate or what I wore and how I felt in it. I remember experiences by how fat I felt, what food I denied, or if I felt thinner than the day before.

My life at school became very stressful and I started needing to plan out restrictions and purges. I began losing weight naturally when I was put on a high energy dance show. Since I hadn't tangibly lost weight in a while, it was like a drug to me, a highly addictive drug. Once again, I began the pursuit of the ideal body.

This is it, I told myself, *I've started dropping weight, I can finally get skinny.*

It seemed so easy at the time. I started restricting more and more, a little more everyday, and the weight kept dropping. The emptiness I felt inside meant I was doing it right. My light-headedness meant I was doing it right. I knew in my deepest heart of hearts this was a bad emotional place for me to be going. I had resisted going there for years.

I remember the day I bought my new scale, my weight loss gum, and set up my free calorie count profile online. I visited Pro-Ana and Pro-Mia websites- websites created by girls wishing to succeed in their eating disorders. These have pages and pages of tips and ways to have a successful eating disorder. I would grin to myself, knowing they'd missed a few tricks. I had a few more. I kept them to myself, knowing I was better at my eating disorder than anyone else. I was winning.

It felt like, for the first time in years, everything was right again. It was like I was cradling a child in my arms that had been looking for me, begging for me to come home. I took it in with wide open arms, soothed it, caressed its face, and brought it into my home and into my heart.

At first it felt good. Opening my scale felt like Christmas. It was the first time I felt excited and clear-headed in what felt like a very long time. I stood on it and didn't care about my friend's and family's voices screaming, "NO!" in my head. I looked down and that was it. I was back. I was hooked.

I weighed myself countless times a day. I found my mind drifting off in class, anticipating the next time I could step on that scale. Those numbers told me everything. They rewarded me, they punished me. They told me exactly who I was everyday. I relied on those numbers to define who I was. My scale told me when I was a *good girl*, that I was succeeding in losing weight. My scale told me when I was a failure if the numbers hadn't dropped. It was an endless game. The number could never be low enough. My best friend, my scale, told me everything I needed to know. It guided everything in my life. Those numbers told me exactly how to get in and out of everyday life. I'd zero it out, step on, watch as it spun, and then stopped. I'd look at the number and that was what defined me. I had a love affair with my scale, it was everything.

I obsessively counted calories. I logged everything I ate online. I spent hours everyday, isolated in my room, calculating burned calories. I stopped eating a wide variety of food. I restricted myself to a rigid diet. If it was a carrot day, I'd eat only carrots. If it was an apples day, I'd eat only apples. I read about a caloric restriction diet, rotating the intake on a daily basis. The lowest day would require 200 calories while the highest 800. Pretty soon, I loved the feeling of the 200-calorie days enough to just stay on this consistently. Not eating more than 200 calories a day.

Digesting. I wasn't digesting more than 200 calories a day. I'd get home at night after exhausting days at school and binge and purge while I did homework until I fell asleep. I stopped going to parties. I stopped hanging out downstairs where many of my classmates would spend evenings together. The days were exhausting.

Piecing it out and trying to make sense of that period of my life, it doesn't add up. I remember being cold. The kind of cold that made me feel as though wet towels were draped all over my body. The kind of cold where I couldn't stop shivering. I started sleeping with socks on my hands, because my hands were so cold it kept me up at night. I remember almost falling asleep in classes, classes that were supposed to mean the world to me. I remember being backstage, going from scene to scene, wrapped in a blanket. I was an exhausted blob, trying desperately to find the energy for the next scene. When I wasn't onstage, I was backstage shivering. When I was onstage, I was trying not to pass out from lack of energy. I was trying to get myself offstage to the next time I could be curled up in my blanket. When I was curled up, I was anticipating my next workout. I was waking every morning to go to the gym, even before dance classes. At night, I'd sneak over to the gym for more. I couldn't get enough. I could finally see the tendons in the backs of my knees- just like the 'skinny girls' on my childhood soccer team.

I watched with delight as the numbers on the face of my scale dropped. Pretty soon, none of my clothes fit me and I had to take myself shopping. As every week went by, I had to go buy new clothes to fit my shrinking body.

My mom, very worried, sent me protein pills. One day, my roommate walked in on me in the kitchen. I was wrapped in a towel after a shower, trying to persuade myself to take a protein pill. It was 15 calories. If I took it, it would ruin everything for the day. My roommate, who was also very worried, hugged me as I sobbed. I knew I needed to take it, but I couldn't put it in my mouth. It was almost as if I didn't know how. If I put it in my mouth, I'd have to chew it, I'd have to taste it, I'd have to swallow it. I'd have to live with the extra calories and the failure.

I couldn't explain to my roommate that I was struggling with an eating disorder. I couldn't explain why I couldn't take the pill. I tried, but I couldn't say anything. My mind just wouldn't allow it. He continued to hug me as I cried.

My mom would call quite often. I was once on the phone with her on a way to an important rehearsal, light headed, as she tried to coach me to drink some juice, just to have something in my system. My mother has a master's in psychology, she is patient and is incredible with positive reinforcement. And she was terrified I was going to die.

"We're going to do this one sip at a time," she'd say.

"Okay," I mumbled, in tears and exhausted.

"Can you lift the glass to your lips and take just one sip? Can you focus on good nourishment?"

"I can't," I sobbed.

"Okay, sweetie, why not?"

"S' gonna make me fat."

"It's going to nourish you, sweetie, it's going to give you energy so you can go to rehearsal."

I held the glass in front of my face and my mind would not allow me to bring it to my lips. The encouragement came from my mother, endlessly, until, "I CAN'T, IT'S GOING TO MAKE ME FAT!" I screamed and hung up the phone.

I desperately wanted to graduate from school and it was still a couple months away. My mother knew those couple months could kill me. My parents tried to take me out of school early to put me in treatment. I fought hard to stay. I had meetings with the director of the school, and my teachers, and promised I'd go into treatment when I graduated. One of my teachers, clueless and loving, noticed how thin I was getting and asked me if I didn't have enough money to buy food. He offered to buy me groceries. I shook my head and couldn't explain.

From this time, I don't remember interactions with people I loved. I remember avoiding people and found many of my closest friends aggravating and I couldn't get away from them fast enough. I remember wanting to die at one point. It seemed easier than trying to find the re-start button in my brain. Once I was in the trap, I couldn't get out. But I was on my way to the ideal body. It was always just a few pounds away.

In this pursuit, I stole food from my roommates, lied to my friends, and continued to abuse my body. I hated myself every second for getting into this mess. I didn't trust my judgement anymore. Someone who was once so organized and enthusiastic had the auto-responses of, "I have no idea… I dunno… I can't take care of that…I don't want to go… I don't care…" I was too tired to care about anything, including my classmates' wellbeing and the pursuit of my career.

Every comment about how thin I was reaffirmed that I was doing it right. Especially when the comments went from, "You look great," to "You're so skinny… you're way too skinny, girl… freakishly thin, you need to eat." The costume department had to alter my costume half-way through the run of a show because it kept falling off while I was onstage.

The thinner I got- the closer I got to my ideal body- the further away it seemed to be. The more I hated my existence, the more I hated myself. My life was completely out of control. The more I tried to control it, the worse it became. I knew exactly what I needed to do to get through each hour of each day, to appease the voice in my head. My eating disorder controlled it all, because I was finally there.

I was thin.

I don't remember when I gave up the ideal body image. It became more of a game. My eating disorder challenged me to see how small I could get. I reached weight goals that my former 'fat' self would never believe possible. It was a test of my strength, my will power, my work ethic. I was finally there and I wanted to die. I could feel my body slowing down, feel my irregular heartbeat, I could feel my insides eating away at themselves. The ideal body didn't exist anymore, I just had to be thin. And thin could always be thinner.

Many times I wished I could go into my brain and hit a restart button. I hated everything about myself. Meanwhile, my life was perfect. I was at the school I always wanted to be at. I had a family of close friends. I was pursuing my life goal. I had dreamed about this heaven my whole life.

I don't remember the last few months of school. I had worked and planned my whole life to get to my beautiful school, to study my passion, and I don't remember the last, most crucial months. I didn't even really acknowledge my graduation from a performing arts school. I walked across the stage, shook hands with the directors of the program, and said goodbye to my classmates. I played a lead in a Shakespeare play. Apparently I did it very well. But all that mattered was watching my mother's face drop when I put on my graduation dress.

"What?"

"Nothing, you're just... so... thin, darling."

Toward the end of my time away at school, my boyfriend and I were watching a movie together when a scene of two people on a date came up on the screen. The movie was a comedy, so my boyfriend was curious why I was suddenly sobbing.

"I'm never going to be able to do that. I'm never going to be able to go out on a date. I'm never going to be normal. I'm never going to be able to eat a meal with someone and be normal. I'm 21 and I'm never going to be able to date. I'll never be able to share a meal with someone, to sit across the table from someone and eat. I'm never going to be normal." I sobbed as he held me.

"You think you should go to treatment, Bud?" He asked, using our nickname for each other.

It had never occurred to me to go to treatment. I never thought I'd be *that* person. I wasn't sick enough to go to treatment. I wasn't disordered enough. I always had it under control. I certainly wasn't thin enough. I would never be thin enough.

I nodded through my tears.

The toll that the pursuit of the ideal body has taken on me is indescribable. No words can do justice to everything my pursuit stripped away from me. It has robbed me of real memories, trust, fun, and health. And the ideal body kept changing, morphing, so it was always just out of my reach. It went from skinny to fit, to sexy, to super-model-thin. Back to fit, back to thin. To no curves, no hips, no breasts, little girl body whose bones are visible, even through her clothing.

I never achieved it. I became thin, but everything the thin body was supposed to bring me, I was mistaken. I was duped. I was misled. I was tricked. I was betrayed by that body. I was not healthy, I was not fit. I was not beautiful. On paper, I was successful in other endeavors, but I never acknowledged my success. I never felt truly successful. When I could've stopped to be proud of myself for real elements of my life, I shrugged it off and let it pass by because I was pursuing the ideal body. I let relationships fall to pieces. It took away everything for nothing. My whole-hearted pursuit left me curled in a ball, with absolutely nothing left to give the world, in exchange for nothing.

The last few months before being admitted into treatment, I was completely numb inside. I went from activity to activity in my life with my eyes glazed over- only thinking about the next time I could exercise, binge & purge, or weigh myself. When it came to being admitted to the treatment facility, the level of potassium in my bloodwork was so low, they couldn't safely admit me for treatment. They wouldn't admit me because I was at too high a risk for a heart attack. This was from the excruciating amount of purging I was engaging in. When throwing up, the body's vital chemicals are purged out along with all of the food.

I got a prescription for a potassium infusion on the Saturday before I was to be admitted into treatment. I needed to boost my levels, so I could be safely admitted to a residential facility, not a hospital or inpatient facility.

That Saturday, I wandered through the halls of a deserted hospital, confused, looking for someone to administer this infusion, and barely caught the woman as she was leaving for her lunch break.

"I need potassium," I said casually, like this happened everyday.

"Excuse me?" she replied.

"I need a potassium infusion," I repeated.

"I can't just give you a potassium infusion," she scoffed.

"I have a prescription and I need it." I half-heartedly lifted the paperwork toward her and started crying. This was the second time I'd been admitted to the hospital for potassium that summer because I couldn't control my purging. "I'm going into treatment for an eating disorder on Monday and they won't admit me until my potassium is higher. Please," I begged.

Her face softened as she said, "I'm sorry, of course, I didn't realize. People don't just wander the halls asking for potassium on a Saturday afternoon," and, trying to make light of it, "Let's see what we can do."

I lay there, helpless, getting pumped full of potassium, my vein burning, trying to sleep, pretending to sleep, crying, pretending to watch the television in front of me. My mom came in and covered my malnourished body with a blanket. I couldn't imagine what it was like to be her in those moments, so powerless against the monster inside my head. I was powerless and it was mine. I had to survive two more nights and then I'd be in the treatment facility. And it was survival. So many times in those last few months I felt my heart palpitating and stutter as though it were going to stop. I'd feel my brain go fuzzy, my vision closing in, my face going numb, and have to brace myself against a wall. I had those experiences every single day.

In those moments in the hospital bed, I realized that the eating disorder had won. I was close enough to death that I was in the hospital getting pumped with fluids. I was tired, I was sick of fighting against it, sick of the voices in my head. I was exhausted and beaten down. I just lay there crying. I was sick of fighting with my family about my eating disorder. Sick of spending all my money on binge food, sick of counting calories, sick of compulsively trying to burn more than I ate. So sick. I was ready to be done.

Two days later, I packed up some clothes, and my parents drove me to the Center for Hope of the Sierras, CHS. When I got there, they did intake paperwork, interviews, took my vitals, and made lunch for me and my family. We were supposed to eat lunch out on the swing on the front porch of my new home. The sandwich was the biggest sandwich I'd ever seen. The girls and I eventually came to joke about these sandwiches. The chef at the Center made them for everyone upon their arrival. We called them Poof Sandwiches, because they sit there, poofing out at you, as you sit there not eating them. They're huge.

The irony was painful. If I could sit on a porch with my family and eat a sandwich, I wouldn't be here. I picked at my Poof Sandwich, and looked at my mom.

"You can relax now, Mom. I'm in good hands. They'll take care of me here, you're done. Thank you for everything." She nodded. My mom worked hard to get me into the Center. I could tell she was beginning to accept that she could never love me enough to take away my eating disorder. She really did everything a mom could do to try and save me from the beast inside me and it still took over.

With that, my parents left me in good hands. I put my armor on and got ready to fight the beast that had plagued me for the last 15 years.

I AM READY TO HEAL MY HEART,
I AM DESERVING OF THIS

My time at the Center for Hope of the Sierras

For the first two weeks, I slept. I slept and cried. I was relieved to finally be in the care of professionals, relieved that I no longer had to hide, no longer had to keep fighting the battle on my own. I was exhausted from hiding, fighting, and starving. I was also terrified. I slept and prepared myself to fight.

I tucked myself into my bed at CHS knowing my friends were in rehearsals for shows I had auditioned for a few months earlier. I was heartbroken, but it solidified that I had made the right decision. At the time of the auditions, I knew I'd be going into treatment after graduation. I politely informed the directors that I would not be available over the summer for rehearsals and performances, and stated, "Please don't cast me, I cannot accept a role. I am just auditioning for practice. Thank you." Looking back now, I'm sure they all knew why.

I felt like a failure when it occurred to me that while my peers would be paying off students loans, I'd be paying off treatment. While my friends laughed, learned, played, and ate, carelessly, I was wrapped in my blanket, eyeing the other girls in treatment- comparing body sizes, thinking how much fatter I was, and wondering if I was truly sick enough to be there. Truly sick enough. I was so pale, colorless, and lifeless, and had such severe bags under my eyes when I arrived at CHS that the other girls thought I was "on drugs."

The harangue of self sabotaging comparisons continued to play in my head. While my peers dream of flying or falling, I'm haunted by nightmares of my fat jeans not fitting, dreams of outgrowing all of my clothing. I have dreams of my loved ones telling me that I've gained weight. I'd think, "*years from now, my peers will go to high school*

26

Career Days to talk about their careers and how successful they are. I will go to high schools and talk about Eating Disorder Awareness."

As my peers grew into adulthood, I took my child sized body and began to untangle the mess I made of myself. I'd watch their social media posts go by, thinking, "*That should be me... I should be working on my career... I should've been in that show... I shouldn't be here... All of their lives look so normal...*"

I'd sit down at the next meal and fight to eat every bite. Every single bite was a painful reminder that I couldn't just go be in a show. Or hold a career. Or go to school. I had to be *here.* I had to try to silence the comparisons and accept that this was not a waste of time. I wasn't wasting precious time I should be spending shaping my career. I was taking time to heal. I would do it now, and never come back.

The Center for Hope of the Sierras, CHS, consisted of two houses, each with up to six girls. I shared a room with two other girls at first and got to switch rooms after having been there for a few weeks. The first week I was there I was on what is called Observation- or OBS for short. OBS means I was under a 24 hour watch by someone on the staff (nurses, resident assistants, therapist). The concept sounds violating, but to me it was comforting knowing that someone was taking care of me, there for me, watching over me every minute of every day. They helped me adjust into my new life in recovery. I requested, and was granted, special permission to go outside to brush my hair. I had to take an RA with me though. Due to severe malnutrition, my hair was falling out in clumps and I didn't want to get it all over the bathroom.

All of the bathrooms at CHS are locked and the RA has to let you in if you have to use the facilities. The RA also has to check the toilet, for evidence of purging, before you flush. Everytime, no matter what. I was extremely constipated upon arrival, so I didn't have to adjust to someone looking at my bowel movement for a few days.

These measures sound violating, and at first, I thought I would have difficulty adjusting, but I found it all comforting. I knew I had reached a point in my life where I couldn't take care of myself and this was the kind of environment I needed to be in. It was comforting and supportive to me.

We ate breakfast at 8:30a, lunch at 12:30p, and dinner at 6:30p, with snacks in between meals. This was an incomprehensible amount of eating for me, as I couldn't remember having a normal eating pattern in my life. At first, I was such a slow eater that it seemed as soon as I was finished with a meal, it was time for a snack. As soon as I was finished with that, it was time for the next meal. It was hell. Someone was always talking about, fixing, or eating food. It was exhausting. It was all food, everything about food, and I was surrounded by girls who were as obsessed with food as I was.

We were able to joke about it with one another.

"All we do now is eat!"

"Is it seriously time to eat again?"

It was all in jest, but the underlying competition was to see who could despise eating the most. She would win, her eating disorder was the best. These competitions seemed to be everywhere; who could eat the slowest, who felt the most full after meals, who was the least hungry before? The RA's kept a very close eye on these competitions and were able to help us identify the eating disorder in our behaviors. They would help us return to recovery oriented attitudes.

We were blind-weighed on Mondays and Thursdays. We'd wake up, put on a thin dressing gown, similar to one you'd wear in a doctor's office, and walk over to where they had the scale. The RA was the only one who had the number. I'd step on the scale and desperately want the RA to tell me what the number was. She'd look at a digital dial in her hand, neutral faced, write the number on a sticky note next to my name, and say, "thank you".

I'd then go get ready for my day wondering how the most exciting part of my life had been reduced to this neutral routine. All while in that stupid little gown. Weighing myself used to be the most climatic part of my day. I was addicted to the ritual of it, it meant everything to me, and feeling it reduced to the neutral-faced routine made me want to grab the sticky note, with the number that I thought defined me, and run. I was desperate to know what the number was. The RA's were hyper aware of this need and they also knew that having that number would be detrimental to my recovery. It was true for any girl there.

The first few weeks at the Center were painful. Emotionally and physically painful. I was accustomed to being empty and, everytime I ate, I felt as though I had a bowling ball in my stomach.

Before and after every meal, we were asked to rate our hunger on a scale from 0-10. A zero, or one, meant 'totally famished, I've never been so hungry in my life.' A ten meant 'Thanksgiving Day stuffed, I've never been so full in my life.' The purpose of the hunger scale was to gauge how much I needed to eat. It also helped after meals in judging if I ate too much or too little. These numbers gave us a structure for our discussions that we had before and after each meal. The discussions took place away from the dining area- the dinner table was not a place to discuss eating disorders. The table was a place for conversations about life and laughter, which often was a nice distraction for those of us who considered the table a battle ground.

In our discussions before each meal, we'd state our hunger level and set goals for ourselves. Mine often consisted of no hunger ("I don't know how I'm going to eat, I'm already stuffed") and setting the goal of, "I'm going to finish my meal within the time limit". My goals morphed through my time in treatment. I became aware of actual hunger and fullness as opposed to emotional fullness. I began setting goals that had to do with my behaviors, (not cutting things into small pieces) and eventually turned into goals like, "I want to taste my dinner tonight."

Post-meal discussions required us to revisit our initial goals and our hunger levels. This was also the time to comment on someone else's behaviors, accomplishments, observations. We got real feedback and gave others feedback as well. Everyone's goals were constantly changing and everyone was in a different stage of their recovery. It was helpful to watch and comment on those who were further along in their recovery, watch their struggles, and how they overcame them at every meal.

These discussions forced me to make connections between my emotions and my thoughts about eating. Eventually, I was able to say things like, "I'm having severe body image issues today. My pants feel tight, and I think it has something to do with my family session this afternoon. I don't feel hungry at all. I hate going into a meal feeling like a 9 and having to eat when I already feel full. My goal is to just get through it and finish my meal."

The discussions were also a time to reflect on our successes. "I feel really good about how I'm doing so far today. I think I did well with both breakfast and lunch. My mind isn't reeling on body image. I think

I portioned myself an appropriate amount. I'm about a 4 and my goal is to listen to my body and stop eating when I'm satiated."

At first, I never knew if I was hungry or not. My hunger signals were disjointed from years of the restrict-binge-purge cycle. However, I did know when there was food in my stomach and it tortured me. I had to get rid of it. It felt like it was trying to claw its way out of my gut. I was desperate to purge. To throw it all up. I could feel every ounce I had eaten. I could feel it expanding in my stomach and therefore expanding my body: my thighs, my stomach, my arms.

But I sat there. I sat there in the discomfort for hours, feeling like a 12 on the hunger scale, facing the emotions that came along with having food in my stomach.

I'd lay there in the living room, groaning, trying to find the most comfortable position to digest. I had severe regurgitation; food would randomly come out of my stomach and into my mouth. I had been throwing up for so long, that's just what my body was expecting. I had to swallow it back down. It was as though I had to keep re-eating my dinner because my bulimic body wasn't accustomed to keeping food in my stomach.

Learning to keep food in my stomach was crucial to recovery. I sat through the torture and all of the emotions that surfaced with having to digest. The emotions came, and instead of vomiting them away, I processed through them. I spoke aloud about every bite making me fat. That "good girls" don't eat. That I don't need food. I am the exception to the rules of humanity. I don't need to eat. I have no needs. Keeping the food in my stomach meant I was gluttonous. Keeping it down meant I was out of control, I'd lost my control. If I lost control and ate, I'd always gain power back by emptying my stomach. Suddenly, without the power to purge, all of my super-powers were gone.

In the early stages of my recovery, my post-meal discussions almost always involved tears for me. "I'm easily an 11 or 12 right now. I've never had so much food in my stomach. I can feel my body swelling up and my jeans getting tighter. I can't even put into words how fat and gross I am." Eventually, I was able to articulate why I felt fat, why I so desperately wanted to throw up, and why I struggled during meals.

In these post meal discussions, the feedback we gave and received from the other residents was invaluable. We were able to call each other out on behaviors that would otherwise slip past, unacknowledged. Our eating disorders were in competition with each other after all and all of us were hyper aware of how the others were behaving..

We were able to discuss these detrimental competitions after a meal once. The meal was nachos, we had to eat them with our hands, and no one finished in the allotted time. "Your eating disorders are competing with each other to see who can be the least hungry and who can be the most full. And who can eat the slowest! I need you girls to stop paying attention to each other's hunger levels and listen to your own damn bodies. You are here to heal. Now allow yourselves to start feeling hunger!"

After that, our pre-meal discussions changed from being competitions to see who could be the least hungry, to genuinely trying to get in touch with our own body's signals. I began to listen to my body and began to allow myself to be below a 5 on the hunger scale.

I began to use other resident's objective reality to combat my eating disorder, and they used mine as well. I'd hear the words, "I know how hard that was for you, I'm so proud of you," from someone I knew understood and it would bring light to the darkness. Someone else's words could illuminate the dark thoughts trying to consume me. We could fight for each other's recovery, secretly knowing that the words we were saying out loud could easily be turned on ourselves.

"I know you feel full right now, but there's no way you've gained any weight from as little food as you just ate. That is your eating disorder screaming at you, and you should be proud of yourself for combating the thoughts in your head. You're taking steps to be able to do normal things. You did good. I noticed you didn't cut your food into tiny pieces today and you finished in time. That means you are fighting. Good job." I started saying "Good job" to whoever I was giving feedback to. It caught on. It kept us recovery oriented.

After a few weeks, my body became accustomed to being fed again and my hunger signals returned. But my eating disorder still wouldn't allow me to admit it. Ever. Because *I don't get hungry*. My eating disorder continued to tell me that skinny girls don't get hungry. The voice in my head told me that if I admitted my hunger then I was no better than a fat, gluttonous pig. I had never allowed myself to admit that I felt hunger. I was better than hunger. I was more powerful than hunger. I don't get hungry. Actually, I'm super-human. I'm in complete control of my body's needs and hunger doesn't exist for me. Hunger is for the weak. These thoughts led my therapists to give me Goal Work regarding my Hunger.

At CHS, I was given weekly assignments called Goals. These were homework assignments based on your own personal struggles and accomplishments. Our Goal Work included journal entries with specific prompts, creative representations (art work), self-care assignments, specific challenges, or analysis of certain situations/experiences. Our Goals helped us outline and articulate our recovery process, which in turn, helped untangle the eating disorder.

I had to continue to eat through the voices in my head screaming at me that I'd never amount to anything if I kept eating, that if I kept eating I was worthless. Voices screaming that I didn't deserve to eat. That I was better than eating.

I had to listen to, and honor, my body. In order to begin honoring my hunger, I went through the motions: pick up the fork, put food on the fork, place it in my mouth, chew, swallow. Repeat. All of this with the eating disorder screaming at me, knowing it is what I'd have to do to recover. I went through the motions to get my life back. At many points in my recovery, I simply resorted to going through the motions, knowing the next physical step, and taking it.

It felt gross, putting food in my mouth. I ate, knowing it was going to stay inside me. There were people around, watching me. It was shameful. I felt like I was letting my eating disorder down. It felt almost as though I had to relearn how to eat, almost like I'd never learned in the first place. The act of nourishing my body and doing it properly were now forgein concepts to me.

Sandwiches were the hardest. Picking up food with my fingers and bringing it toward my face, putting it in my mouth. It felt like I was shovelling food into my face.

"Eew, Mom. Gross."

I felt as though I needed to apologize, I have no idea to whom, for putting a sandwich in my mouth. I'd take a bite and quickly bring my other hand up to cover my face as I chewed, slowly. I felt like no one should have to watch me chew this. It felt disgusting, but we ate sandwiches several times a week, there was no avoiding it. I became better at it; bringing food up to my mouth, placing it in my mouth, and eventually chewing and swallowing without apology.

I was assigned many memorable, enlightening, Goals while at CHS. One required me to actually research the human digestive system. I'm a well-educated, straight-A student, who paid attention in science and anatomy classes, but my eating disorder had me convinced that everything I put in my mouth was piling up in the form of pockets of fat- all over my body. Like a game of Tetris. I cried, sobbed, through meals convinced that every bite I put in my mouth was accumulating and I was getting fat again.

I had worked hard to get skinny, I had worked hard for my eating disorder, and now I was messing it all up. I envisioned the inside of my body as a river of sludge and fat. I envisioned that everything I ate would float down this river and get trapped on the sides. This fatty sludge would just pile up on all the fatty pockets already there. I felt it accumulating, making me fat. I thought the inside of my body was made up of fat-pockets piling up like a child's building blocks.

This image haunted me during and after every meal. My Goal was to research the human metabolic system and disprove my eating disorder's Tetris Theory. I had to research and prove to myself that most of the food I was putting in my body was actually getting converted into energy and getting used by my body for vital processes- not piling up as fat. I had to start to believe that food is fuel for my body and necessary. For the time being, food was medicine.

One of the most difficult meals we had at CHS was Sloppy Joes. While each of us cringed with every bite, the RA's desperately encouraged us to pick these messy buns up with our hands and eat them like "normal". We refused and continued to eat them elegantly, properly-with forks and knives. Half-way through the meal, I had to get up and wash my hands- not because I was messy, I didn't have a speck of Joe on me, but because I felt disgusting from eating this particular meal.

That night, the post-meal discussion stretched out for almost an hour as we discussed what types of foods we associate with what types of people. And why we refrain from eating those foods: because we do not want to be associated with those types of people. My eating disorder associated Sloppy Joes with a lazy, obese culture.

"It's in the name!"

The Sloppy Joe battle uncovered connections to a culture we'd all desperately been trying to detach ourselves from. A fat-phobic culture of obesity. We wanted nothing to do with it. Every girl in the room felt that we were now a part of that culture for eating this specific meal.

"We're sloppy now!"

We felt terrible. We had all betrayed our eating disorders. The nurse on duty at the time found our associations fascinating and helped us dig deeper into these mental heuristics.

"Both of my kids love Sloppy Joes. My friends love Sloppy Joes. Are you afraid of being associated with my kids? Are you afraid of being associated with my friends?"

We all shook our heads "no".

"There is nothing about a meal, nothing about a certain food, that is going to force you to be labeled as lazy, glutinous, or sloppy. Do not let your eating disorders win this battle. Do not allow yourself to be labeled good or bad based on the meal you just ate."

With recovery in mind, I allowed myself to take these words to heart. That I can eat foods in moderation without becoming obese. I began exploring what it would be like to enjoy foods, even finger foods, even messy foods, without being labeled lazy or gluttonous. That these labels are all in my head. I can eat all types of food without worrying that people will think I'm messy, lazy, fat, or sloppy.

We were presented with different challenges like this every single day. Wednesdays were Out to Lunch days and Fridays were Snack Challenge. Snack Challenge included going to a grocery store and picking out a snack that challenged the eating disorder in some way. For example, a candy bar. One day, I chose a fruit tart. We would take these snacks back to the Center and eat them there.

At first, this challenge made no sense to me and made me furious.

"I don't see how eating a stupid candy bar is going to help me get over my eating disorder," I'd protest, "I can't even eat a regular meal. Don't force feed me candy, this is so dumb."

But this challenge was about more than just eating a candy bar. It was about the entire experience of going to a grocery store and choosing something to eat. Choosing it knowing that you'd have to eat it.

Choosing it based on hunger levels, what sounded good, what was available. It was about developing the ability to eat in any situation. The Snack Challenge helped me develop the ability to find anything to eat, in any situation. Not in a survival sense, but in an everyday lifestyle sense. It taught me how to listen to and take care of my needs without having the eating disorder commandeer the situation and not let me eat anything at all. Previously, I'd freeze up in grocery stores. I had stopped allowing myself to purchase anything other than negative calorie foods or binge/purge food. I bought food only for purging. Knowing I had to eat something and keep it down, was terrifying. I'd freeze up, not knowing how to make decisions, forget what I was doing, not able to listen to my body. I'd panic and not even know what I was looking at.

Snack Challenge was important training for me to exist in a real world and not be ruled by my eating disorder. Being out and about in my everyday life, being able to take care of myself, and not ignore my needs. I learned how to simply be able to grab a snack when I was hungry and establish myself as a real person.

The Snack Challenge grew easier with time, as most things do. Most of my time in treatment, and recovery, was a process of panicking, doing the right behavior, calming down, panicking, remembering how I handled it last time, doing the next right behavior, and calming down.

Once, we went to a cupcake cafe, the girl working the counter asked if we were some sort of sorority. We giggled and one of our girls rolled her eyes, "Something like that."

A few weeks into treatment my therapists witnessed a beautiful phenomenon reveal itself within me. The therapists at CHS love watching The Lift of the Brain Fog. About two weeks into treatment, they watch as the residents begin to form more intelligent, more coherent sentences. They watch the levels of intelligence in sessions, and in daily life, rise as the brain becomes properly nourished. They watch creativity and conversation increase. I was no exception.

After being in treatment for a few weeks, feeding myself consistently, my brain began to function again. After getting proper nourishment, my "foggy brain" disappeared and I was able to form coherent thoughts and sentences. Due to malnourishment, my brain had been foggy for years, I had just become used to it. The relief of being in treatment, the proper nutrients, the ability to start disentangling my eating disorder; all of this led to my eyes brightening up, my enthusiasm to contribute in group sessions, and my increased creativity and self-exploration.

Another phenomenon I experienced was my metabolism turning into a furnace as I consistently gave it fuel. I actually started losing weight when I began eating again and the dietician had to keep increasing my caloric intake.

At first when she really had to start increasing the amount of food I was eating, my dietician asked me, "Have you been doing anything different with food in the last few days?"

I squirmed. I thought I was being punished. I thought I was ballooning up out of control and the dietician wanted to know why. I admitted sheepishly that I'd had a piece of banana bread. My eating disorder started whirling in my head, "See, even the dietician thinks you're getting fat. Too fat. She's gonna tell you you're fat enough now and can go home!"

"I only ask because you are losing weight," she said.

I couldn't help the grin that spread across my face. I was still in control, I was still the thinnest.

"We're going to have to start increasing the amount you're eating. We'll do it slowly, you won't even notice the difference in the amounts on your plate."

It seemed like everyday I went to my plate there was a larger pile of food than the day before. I had to fight my eating disorder every moment of every meal, with the help of the RA's. I put every ounce of my mental energy into developing an objective reality for myself. A reality where the amount of food had not increased as much as my eating disorder was telling me.

My eating disorder was telling me how huge the pile of food was because I was a *fat, gluttonous pig.*

My recovery-oriented mind fought back with *'it's slightly more food than yesterday because my body is using the fuel and needs more of it.'* I fought with my misperceptions and misinterpretations of reality, so as not to give my eating disorder any power back.

Until the morning when bagels were served for breakfast. After the pre-meal discussion, I walked to my spot at the table. Where there was normally half a bagel, there was an entire bagel. I looked at the RA with panic in my eyes. She looked at me apologetically and said, "I'm sorry, I should've warned you."

I was eating four times longer than any of the other girls that morning. Everyone sat there in silence watching me eat, grateful that they were not the ones having to eat the entire tear-soaked bagel.

Suddenly, I was the fattest girl at the table. I was the fattest I have ever been. Every bite was piling up. Every bite was making me fat again. I was fat, I was sloppy, I was ugly. One of the girls got up and put music on to encourage me to finish eating, to take my mind off of the bagel, and to help silence the eating disorder screaming at me. The other girls could hear the shame reverberating in my head.

The song was Martina McBride's "This One's For The Girls." The music worked. The lyrics pulled me out of my eating disorder and gave me the inspiration to finish the bagel. I was reminded why I was here, in treatment. The music encouraged me to continue eating.

This one's for the girls,
Who've ever had a broken heart;
Who've wished upon a shooting star;
You're beautiful the way you are.

This one's for the girls,
Who love without holding back,
Who dream with everything they have,
All around the world,
This one's for the girls.

Suddenly every bite was more empowering. I ate the bagel for the girls. My housemates were patient with me, my sacred witnesses on my battlefield, as I won another one.

We discussed it afterward in the living room. They knew how challenging it was for me to finish the entire bagel. "You did great. That's normal, you know. Most people eat a whole bagel, not just half. By eating the whole thing, you beat your eating disorder at this meal." I nodded silently. My brain was exhausted and drifting far from where I was sitting on the couch, wondering how I was going to get through this day, suddenly 20 lbs heavier.

I wanted to be normal. I wanted the beast out of my head. Getting there was painful. It meant doing things that seemed to me like the end of the world. It meant taking actions that tore me up inside, actions that ruined my skinny-identity. I did all of these things trusting that I would be normal someday.

I did not gain 20lbs from the bagel. In fact, I got another calorie bump a few days later because I had lost even more weight.

If I thought I had been eating a lot when I was first admitted to the Center, I was very mistaken. By the fourth week of treatment this is what my eating schedule looked like:

6:30a Snack
8:30a Breakfast
10:30a Snack
12:30p Lunch
3:30p Snack
6:30p Dinner

My calorie intake stayed steady then. I had to eat normal amounts of food from that day forward without my eating disorder coming in and high-jacking my brain. This one was for the girls, for everyone struggling. I did not want to struggle anymore.

I had a list of reasons to eat, reasons to fight. Everyone did. We all knew each other's motivations for defeating our eating disorders. When someone was struggling, we would remind each other of our reasons to recover. My greatest motivation was that I wanted to date. I wanted to be able to go out on a date. Whenever I was struggling and the eating disorder seemed to be winning a battle, one of the other girls would re-mind me, "You want to date. If you want to be able to date, you have to be able to eat like a normal person." I'd nod and continue to fight as hard as I could. Sometimes these were little tiny goals, like a reason to put an avocado on a salad; "because it's good for your hair." These were seemingly tiny and insignificant, but each was a tiny battle in a huge war. Each battle I won counted against the eating disorder.

Because I was getting proper nutrients, my hair stopped falling out. I hadn't been able to brush my hair without huge clumps of it falling out in about a year. Along with many other ailments from malnutrition, I had chosen to ignore this and hardly ever brushed or washed my hair-just tied it up in a ponytail. When I started eating again, my hair stopped falling out.

I remember running out into the living room one morning, pleased as I'd been since I arrived. "I'm going to straighten my hair," I announced, "It stopped falling out, I can use my straightener now!" The RA's applauded and I couldn't stop smiling.

This was one of my first tangible victories against the eating disorder, one of the first signs of me coming back to life. I was able to brush, straighten, and style my hair. I styled it every morning after that for the remainder of my stay.

Before treatment, I drank a couple pots of coffee a day. I drank coffee as an alternative to eating. I drank coffee as an appetite suppressant. My relationship with coffee was very intertwined with eating disordered behaviors.

While in treatment, I pined for the four days a week that we got coffee. Coffee outings were our reward for finishing meals in the allotted time. Coffee was a privilege that I only lost once. But these exciting days came with many rules. I was allowed one small cup, no refills. I always got my coffee with a bit of half-and-half and a packet of splenda. I savored the cup all afternoon. I'd make a tiny cup of coffee last for hours. At first, I followed all of the rules at CHS, I was perfect. I struggled finishing meals in the allotted time, but I would do almost anything for coffee. Like I said, I only lost my privileges once.

There were a lot of rules at the Center. After my discharge I started to think that part of recovery is learning how to break rules, perhaps that's why there were so very many of them. That the therapists secretly wanted us to start thinking for ourselves, to start thinking outside societal rules and prescriptions.

I made a very important discovery about myself while abiding by all these rules (trying to be perfect), and for the first time in my life, I started breaking rules. The rebellious behaviors were inconsequential, but very important for me.

My whole life, I felt like I had to be perfect. I had to be the perfect little girl. I was a "good girl." When I was in the safe environment of

CHS, I began breaking rules. I began finding a personality of my own, an identity outside of societal expectations. I was finally encouraged to find something other than the perfectionist inside me. And I started breaking rules.

I'd sneak downstairs early in the mornings and drink the RA's coffee when they weren't looking. I'd hide gum in my sock drawer (thanks for the contraband, Mom!) and pass it out to the girls on the way to the movie theatres on Friday nights. I discovered that if I went up to a barista and asked for a "warmer", they'd often just refill the entire cup for me- instead of just heating it back up. I'd do this while the RA wasn't looking and end up with two cups of coffee instead of just the regimented single cup. I was developing critical thinking skills that I had never been en- couraged to develop before. These seemingly inconsequential experiences helped me develop a new identity, one of a creative, empow- ered young woman who can think outside the box.

One of these instances still leaves me giggling to this day. We had a cinnamon-sugar mix on the table that we were allowed to shake onto cereal or breakfast items. But, because many women had a history of us- ing cinnamon as an appetite suppressant, the mix was mostly sugar, and tasted really bad. At this point in my recovery process, I didn't care that the mix was mostly sugar, I just cared that the ratio was off because it tasted gross. We devised a plan to fix the cinnamon-sugar blend. One day one of the girls distracted the RA by asking for something in the garage. This was risky because the residents were never left alone, espe- cially in the kitchen. There were always nurses, therapists, RA's around so we wouldn't be unattended in the kitchen. This day there was only one RA on duty and she went to the garage with our decoy, leaving us to run to the pantry, grab the cinnamon, and pour it as fast as we could into the mix that was mostly sugar. The RA entered back into the dining area as we finished cleaning up our mess. We were all laughing, with huge smiles on our faces. We swelled with astonishment and pride at what we had just gotten away with. We giggled every time someone used the mix from that day on.

Up until I started breaking these simple rules, I was a good girl. I was a perfectionist. I never questioned anything, I followed directions perfectly, I worked hard to please everyone around me. Breaking rules was a huge piece of my recovery. It allowed me to find my own identity outside of the one pushed onto me from family and the pressures society. In return, it gave me the power to break the rules of the eating disorder.

I LET GO OF EVERYTHING WHICH I NO LONGER NEED

Experiencing the stages of grief related to the loss of the eating disorder

One of my Goals while in treatment was to address the grief I was experiencing with the loss of the eating disorder. My eating disorder was my best friend, a loved one, and losing it caused me to feel deep denial, depression, bargaining, much anger, and eventually acceptance.

There were many times when I didn't want to go through with recovery, times when I didn't want to recover. I wanted to keep my eating disorder because it was familiar to me. I went through stages where I knew I needed to get rid of my eating disorder, but I had to continually remind myself why.

> Because it's life threatening.
> *But it made me thin.*
> Because it didn't let me have any friends.
> *But it made me thin.*
> Because it took all my energy and made me cold all the time.
> *But it made me thin.*

While bargaining, I desperately wanted to hang onto my eating disorder. I found myself negotiating my recovery in my head.

Well, I'll get rid of it now, accomplish a few things, and I can always have it later. I can always come back.

I wanted to keep having an eating disorder for just a couple more months. I believed there was so much we didn't get to do together. I wanted to take my eating disorder to another college or starve my way into another tiny costume. I wanted to parade my little body around on another stage, or go dancing and get attention for being thin. I felt like I wasn't ready to let it go.

Then, I wanted to get rid of some of it, but not all of it.

I will stop doing such-and-such behaviors if I can just keep counting calories or weighing.

I promise I'll eat "this" much everyday, if I can just keep weighing myself.

But recovery meant working to get rid of all of the behaviors. I could not stay attached to a few rituals, one or two eating disordered behaviors would eventually allow the rest back in. I had to eliminate all of the behaviors from my life.

Denial came along with bargaining. I denied that anyone knew how to take care of my body better than I did- even the doctors and dieticians. I denied I actually even had a problem. I believed that my behaviors, and relationship with my eating disorder, would fix the problems. I had faith in the eating disorder. I denied that my time at the Center would really help anything. I was so wrapped up in my eating disorder, I believed that disordered behaviors would save me from my eating disorder.

I began to wrap my head around the fact that I was grieving. I found that my eating disorder was like a child inside of me. She wanted attention and desperately sought approval. This child had found ways to cope when she didn't get what she wanted. I was able to calm her. I was able to get attention for her. The behaviors led others to flatter me.

> "Aren't you going to eat?"
> "Is that all you're having?"
> "Are you starving yourself, Bri?".

This child fit in with the pretty girls, or her friends, when they talked about losing weight.

> "Oh, I've been on that diet, try blah, blah, blah."
> "I feel so fat today."
> "You feel fat, look how fat I am."

This child got approval from my mother when she was successful with a diet. I could care for her, take care of her needs, and do her justice by using eating disordered behaviors. I could get attention for her whenever she needed it.

The eating disorder took on a personality. She was demanding and told me exactly how to soothe the crying child inside of me: lose weight, be perfect, keep track of everything you've eaten, look and act like the adults, know everything, don't fail. She was a constant judge in my head coaching me through every day. I was very much entangled in this mess. By soothing her demanding voice in my head, I was soothing her; soothing the crying child inside of me who felt like she never got enough attention, never fit in, and would never be lovable.

When I began my process of recovery, I felt that by disobeying these voices, I was abandoning this child. I felt I was abandoning myself. I became depressed mourning the loss of something I kept so close to my heart for most of my life. My depression turned into an overwhelming hopelessness, as I did not know what my future would look like without my eating disorder. I mourned the friendship I had with my eating disorder and the role it played in my life. My eating disorder was always there for me; my best friend, my playmate when I felt isolated. Something that was mine and no one else's. I went to it for comfort and reassurance.

In recovery, I began stripping away that sense of comfort that my eating disorder had always provided me. I had to admit to myself that there was nothing comforting within the disorder in the first place. I had misled myself into believing a lifelong dream that didn't exist. This dream was the Pursuit of the Ideal Body. The ideal body didn't exist, it was always just out of my reach. It was always just a few pounds away.

I was grieving the loss of a lifelong dream, a dream that never existed in reality. This dream had always been real to me, and I began accepting the loss. I grew up telling myself that I could do anything I wanted to do. I told myself I could accomplish any goal, and the Pursuit of the Ideal Body was the goal I focused all of my energy on. This goal began to dissipate. This goal was no longer an option.

I became angry that I had been misled for all these years. Angry for the loss of a life that could have been spent doing other things or developing a healthy life. Angry that I wasn't a carefree child. Angry that I spent my adolescence with my head in a toilet. Angry that I didn't have the years at college that everyone spoke of as the "time of their lives". Angry for how much I sacrificed for the eating disorder, how much it took away from me.

Angry that my, "shooting for the stars" brought me to the top of the world for a few moments and then crashing down again because the eating disorder always told me, "you can do better," "that wasn't good enough," "this isn't as good as it should be," "you can get thinner." I was always thrust back into the hell to pursue the high of weight loss once again. It was the only way to soothe the voices in my head.

I had to have a blind-trust in the process of treatment and recovery. I began to understand that I had tried the eating disorder as a way-of-life and it only made me miserable, sick, and out of control. I had no choice but to try recovery as a way-of-life and see where it led me.

I sifted through the aspects of my life and discovered that my eating disorder had ruined all of them. I had to accept years of wasted energy, time, money, and relationships. I had to let go of the anger. I had to accept that the eating disorder is not my friend, looking out for my best interests. I had to accept that the eating disorder was no longer serving me- it was no longer a coping mechanism I could rely on. I had to accept that there would always be people in my life who are more fit than me. There will always be people who are thinner than me. I do not have to be the best at everything I do. I am still in the acceptance stage to this day.

Even after years in recovery, I would still experience the grief and the loss of my eating disorder. Every so often, I would miss it. I would miss the consistency. I would miss feeling like I had something concrete to hold onto. I would miss the self-destruct button that was mine and no one else's. But I understand now that it will never be worth all of the sacrifices I had to make to appease the voices in my head.

I WILL NOT LABEL MYSELF AS THE PROBLEM, I AM NOT MY EATING DISORDER

The world through the lens of an eating disorder

Most of my thoughts, especially when I first arrived in treatment were eating disordered. I believed this was normal, as I had had these thought patterns for most of my life. Everything from how I thought about food, to how I carried myself in the world, to how I interacted with other people was dictated by the eating disorder. I had to begin to recognize and distinguish the differences between eating disordered thoughts and thoughts based in objective-reality. Objective-reality is what is actually happening- what is the logical reality.

At first, every thought I had was eating disordered. For example, I'd be trying to add up calories I was consuming while calculating my metabolic rate to be sure I was burning everything off. These pervasive, consistent thoughts were completely normal for me. Spending what seemed like hours looking at and reading labels in grocery stores was normal for me. Making every decision in my life based on calories and food fears was normal for me. Using gum as an appetite suppressant or obsessing over the calorie counts were completely normal behaviors, and habits, for me. This was how I lived my life, how my brain operated, how I existed. Always trying to find the next place to exercise, cutting up food into tiny pieces, making excuses not to eat, rationalizing between eating now or later, or "if I eat today, I won't eat tomorrow." All of these racing thoughts were normal to me. I had become used to them spiraling in my head. And, of course, the most pervasive thought was classifying myself as good or bad based on what I was eating or not eating.

As I began to disentangle these thoughts, I began to realize that I see the world differently than the people around me because I have an eating disorder. My brain works differently because I have an eating disorder.

My world is colored through the lens of an eating disorder. This means that my brain alters everything in the world around me and changes it so I hear something negative about myself, my body, my behaviors, and my capabilities. Even compliments are misconstrued and used as an excuse for me to lose weight.

The eating disorder interprets the world for me. Like a pair of colored glasses, every word, every thought, every situation is run through the lens of my eating disorder and then interpreted in my brain. My eating disorder operated as a filter to process and internalize the external stimuli in my world. Everything I hear other people say is interpreted as a negative narrative toward my body or behaviors around food. For example, a person could be talking about something completely unrelated and my eating disorder will hear, "you're fat," "you need to stop eating," "you shouldn't be eating that". This constant self-destructive narrative would lead me to engage in behaviors to change the shape of my body or control its needs. I had to radically accept that I see, and interpret, the world differently than others because I have an eating disorder.

Once I realized this, and noticed how often it happened (every second of everyday), I was able to start separating myself out from the voices in my head. Once I was able to articulate that *I see the world through the lens of the eating disorder,* I was able to start actively taking power away from the enemy.

I questioned every single thought I had. I became insatiably curious about my thought patterns and if I really see the world *that* differently. I'd say these thoughts out loud and ask the other residents and therapists if the thought was 'eating disordered' or 'normal'. I'd write them down and evaluate if someone without an eating disorder would have the same thoughts. I separated myself out from every thought, motivation, and behavior I had, questioning if it had been filtered by my eating disorder or not. I had to continue talking about these thoughts. Verbalizing them, hearing myself say them outloud, and getting feedback was a huge step in separating myself out.

This curiosity led me to stop classifying myself as good or bad based on food choices. I stopped allowing eating disordered thoughts to rule my behaviors. I started acting on self-nurturing thoughts, not self-destructive ones. I didn't have to believe what my eating disorder was telling me, and I certainly didn't have to act on it. When I felt like a good or bad person, based on my food choices, I would be honest and either write it down or talk to someone about it. These discussions helped me solidify that my core values and my core worth were not based on what I was eating.

This is made challenging by the media we surround ourselves with. I began noticing the eating disordered thoughts and behaviors in magazines, television, and other media. It became easier to pinpoint my own disordered thoughts as I analyzed my surroundings as well. I could see it in the idolization of appetite suppression and glorification of weight loss. I began noticing ads that capitalized on, and glamorized, my disordered thinking.

We saw an ad for chewing gum where a woman is walking past a display of cookies in a bakery. As she eyes them longingly, she takes a piece of gum out of her pocket and slips it into her mouth. A woman's voice says, "You're such a good girl." This ad was a living example of the thoughts that were always racing through my head. And further proved to me that I was bad or good based on my food choices and that our society values those who can avoid eating all together.

It was hard to separate myself out from this culture and gain a new perspective because my eating disorder made me feel like I was in control of something everyone else was desperately fighting for control over. My eating disorder let me be "on top of the game." The illusion of control led me to purge everything I ate, hardly eat at all, never admit to hunger, and be in control of my needs. My eating disorder made me feel like I had beaten everyone at a game we were all supposed to be struggling with as women. And my eating disorder was glamorized everywhere. Because I was thin, it was glamorized. I know this is not the case for everyone struggling in an emotional relationship with food. Using food to deal with emotions is disordered eating and is mentally excruciating. It should be treated as such.

Labeling the lens in my head, recognizing the filter, and accepting that my brain operates differently gave me a sense of self outside of the eating disorder and helped me begin to cope and disentangle myself.

THE MOST TERRIFYING THING TO DO
IS ACCEPT ONESELF COMPLETELY

Radical acceptance of self

My history, combined with my eating disorder made me believe that if I wasn't the best at something, or perfect, it wasn't worth doing at all. It was exhausting to be paralyzed by the anxiety of knowing I'll never be perfect. I was always trying to be perfect at everything. I was always trying to know everything, get everything right, and never make any mistakes. The eating disorder fed this black and white thinking and plagued me for years. I needed to be perfect. I needed to be the thinnest, the prettiest. I always needed to be the best. My life was a constant competition with not only those around me, but with myself. Even my relationships and friendships were competitions, I always felt threatened by those around me who may be smarter, prettier, or more capable.

My perfectionism has always been a deeply ingrained need and my eating disorder was another outlet for this perfectionism. The two supported each other in every dysfunctional way possible. I've always had the need to appear perfect, to never make mistakes, to never ask questions, to always have the right answer and know everything.

As a child and into my adulthood, I excelled at most everything I did. I had straight A's, I was well spoken, and mature. I was a good athlete and a talented actor, and always having to be the best at everything took its toll on me. The mindset of having to be the best plagued me constantly and made me believe that "If I can't do it perfectly, why even try?"

While in recovery, I began to accept that I cannot be the best at everything. I realized how much disappointment and wasted energy came along with perfectionism. Reflecting on myself and my life, I was able to accept that I always give my best effort. I started to accept that if I know I am doing my best, that's all I can ask of myself. This has been a long, ongoing, process of accepting, and appreciating, my efforts.

Letting go of perfectionism was accompanied by a lot of shame. Shame, and fear, that I am not good enough. I learned to accept who I am and what I contribute. Though I continued to feel the nagging desire for perfection, I started to let go of the need to be perfect at everything.

I practiced saying, "I don't know." I envisioned myself letting go of the competitive nature and just existing. I started trying to pay attention to the experience instead of the appearance.

Many lengthy therapy sessions and recovery oriented choices made me realize that trying to be perfect, instead of being present in an experience, is not the way I want to live my life. It is not the way I want to be perceived in this world. If I'm constantly trying to be perfect, I will never be able to appreciate efforts that are good enough, efforts that are great. I needed to start appreciating my best. I needed to unwrap myself from the perfection of it all to appreciate the tiny things, the beautiful accomplishments along the way.

Radical acceptance also meant letting go of the dreams the ideal body promised me. It meant digging deep into what I thought it meant to be thin. My eating disorder had me believing that the thinner I was, the more jobs I'd get, the more people would want to hang out with me and spend time around me. Being thin meant more respect. To get out of this trap I had to define what type of people I wanted in my life and began radically accepting that most people do not have the same judgments I do about the size of my body. My objective reality began to take shape and I started accepting that most people are apathetic about the size of my body. I began radically accepting that if someone cared enough about the size of my body to have me risk my health, I did not want to associate with that person. If someone wanted me to risk my well-being to change my body, I did not need that person's presence in my life. I began wanting to surround myself with people who respect me for my behavior, not my body size. I began wanting to manifest the company of people who want to approach me because of my energy, my personality, and my charisma instead of my jean size.

I slowly began giving up the pursuit of the ideal body in exchange for radical acceptance of who I actually am. Knowing what the eating disorder took away from me, and how dysfunctional I became in it's grips, I knew that I could never hold a steady job and be my best, most responsible person while trying to pursue the ideal body. I could never be my outgoing, loving self while engaging in eating disordered behaviors.

My recovery morphed and revealed two choices: pursue the ideal body, just like I had been, and become a dysfunctional being, or let go of this pursuit and achieve real goals- become a wholistic, loving, and caring person. The sacrifices I made to pursue the ideal body were never worth what it took away from me. The eating disorder took away everything good in my life. It took away love and compassion. It took away family, friends, and relationships. It took away my desire to live a life. It took away everything except the brutal pursuit of the ideal body, and it was never worth it.

I remembered what I'd have to endure, once again, to have this ideal body. I remembered the misery and made a very clear choice that it is not worth the sacrifices. I made the choice, the commitment to myself to recover and never go back. I began believing that it is worth my time and effort to accept my body as it is when I am healthy and take care of myself. Accept it and not try to change it. It is worth it to radically accept the body that I am in when I am eating when I'm hungry and stopping when I'm full. I can put all that effort into a life without an eating disorder. I can have a life full of family, friends, goals, and tangible, real, elements.

Every time I made a recovery oriented decision, it took power away from the eating disorder. Every time I chose to accept my body, and my mind, just as I am, I moved closer to being free from the monster.

I learned that there is a difference between the phrases "I can't" and "I won't". As I went through treatment and the eating disorder began to lose power, I felt it losing its grip on me. The refusal to recover, the "I can't" turned into "I won't", and eventually it turned into "I'll try."

When I was in the tight grips of the eating disorder, I'd say, "I can't eat that," "I can't sit still," "I can't keep it down." I felt that I was powerless, that there were things I couldn't possibly do. "I can't" highlights this powerlessness, a surrender to the eating disorder, still completely under its control. "I can't" is a refusal to recover.

As I progressed through treatment, I began saying, "I won't eat that", indicating that the eating disorder still had a hold on me and my decision making, but I was making the choice. The eating disorder was no longer making my decisions. I was making my decisions. It was losing its grip on me. I had free will.

Through this time I was still grasping onto the eating disorder, I was making the decisions, but I was still relying on the eating disorder because it was all I knew. When my decision making became completely recovery oriented, I began to say, "I'll try."

"I'll try to eat that."

The more I stated, "I'll try," the more recovery oriented I became. I began seeking out challenges, things that I could "try". The distance between me and my eating disorder began to grow. Even on the days when the distance was minimal, there was a separation.

There is a lot of trying. The day my skinny jeans didn't fit, I tried and failed. The day the bagel was presented to me, I tried and succeeded.

Recovering from an eating disorder is a long, fierce, war. It is a war made up of many battles. I won some and I lost some, but I kept trying. As long as I was trying, and winning more than losing, I was on the path to recovery. I began trying to radically accept who I am.

I AM GRATEFUL FOR ALL THE THINGS MY BODY ALLOWS ME TO DO.

Redefining my relationship with athletics

A huge piece of my eating disorder was athletics and exercise. A huge piece of my identity was athletics as well, so I had to begin to redefine my relationship with exercise. In order to do this, I began to outline, and analyze, why athletics are so important to me.

Exercise has always been an obligation of mine and something I never felt I could get enough of. I was always striving to be better, faster, stronger. I always felt guilty for not exercising enough. While I was exercising, I always wanted to go faster, harder, longer, and be stronger. Exercise was my permission for everything in my life: to have fun later that day, to eat. Exercising gave me permission to exist without the gnawing guilt. I felt like if I didn't exercise enough in a week, I was letting myself down. I would feel extremely guilty for "not taking care of myself," not living up to my own impossible standards. I was "letting myself go."

Any kind of physical activity was my key to feel free to have a good day and rid myself of the burden of having to exercise. I focused on burning calories, and I deeply believed that exercise kept me from getting fat.

While I was ruled by the eating disorder, much of my athletics were a burden. I exercised in order to feel significant or worthy. I had a quota for the day and anything below the quota led to feelings of worthlessness. In the past, I based a good deal of my self-worth on how much activity I was getting, and how hard I pushed myself during that activity. I truly believed that I was only worth how much I was exercising and how thin it was going to make me.

In the past, exercise had always been a way to burn calories and a way to "stay in shape." Feeling "in shape" put me in a place of power. Exercise made me more powerful. Exercise made me feel disciplined, gave me something to work at, something to be good at, and gave me something to obsess about. Going to the gym always felt like I was "doing the right thing." I could unhealthily compete with myself to be better than yesterday. Activities, including track and field, were fraught with competition that gave me palpable goals, gave me something to do and focus on. These goals made me feel significant. It was also a way to burn calories and feel worthy.

I have a memory of my dad and I running together in elementary school. We had gone to the track at the junior high school to train for The Mile. Every year, the school was required to time the kids running a mile and I wanted a "good" time on my mile that year. We were running laps at the track and as I ran past the high jump pit I heard someone sneer in my direction, "Yeah, run off all that fat." I finished my mile in 7:19 that year. Pretty good for a 'fat' 5th grader. But these are the memories that haunted, and motivated, me. Those were the comments that fueled my eating disorder as a child.

I always felt I could run harder, could always be stronger. Running was addicting. I could push myself until it really hurt and then feel stronger the next day. Running made me feel worthy. The worse it hurt, the harder I was pushing myself. The harder I pushed myself, the more deserving I became. Running was an addiction, an outlet for the feelings of worthlessness. And of course, running made me feel thin.

Exercise had always been a way to get in touch with my superior work ethic and see how much I could accomplish if I tried. It had been a release of pent up energy. I felt that if I could be better than others at athletics, I was a better person. Sweating reminded me that I was burning calories. It was a compulsion, an obligation, that made me feel whole. I felt I couldn't accomplish anything worthy without exercise- regardless of how my body actually feels.

My eating disorder fit perfectly into all of this. It was entrenched in everything about my relationship with exercise. It turned exercise into a way to burn off anything I ate. My eating disorder didn't care if I was having fun, it all became about burning calories and trying to feel skinny. Exercise was my redemption for eating, for feeling unsuccessful, or for feeling fat.

When I was in an emotional crisis, feeling upset, panicky, or negative about myself, I thought that the only way to make myself feel better was to burn calories, to exercise. I thought that if I could just fix the way I feel about my body, my state of mind would improve. If I could only run fast enough, pedal hard enough, do enough situps and pushups, I could weight-lift the emotion away.

While in treatment, I was not allowed to exercise at all. I wasn't even allowed to walk up the driveway to say goodbye to my parents when they came to visit. The 30 second walk was considered "over-exercising". Taking away my ability to exercise stripped me of my ability to make myself feel worthy, to validate myself, to alleviate my guilt for existing.

The lack of exercise was even more challenging, because I've always considered myself an athlete. My athletics are a huge piece of my identity and how I define myself. I desperately needed to redefine my relationship with exercise because I needed to have it in my life without being ruled by the eating disorder. It was important not to exercise in order to find my self-worth and a new identity outside of my athletics. I had to know that I was worthy, that I existed, without exercise.

So, I sat in a comfy chair and made friendship bracelets, drew pictures, and worked on my Goals. I sat and laughed with the other residents, played games, and journaled. I didn't exercise for months. I began developing a new identity that didn't include or revolve around physical activity. I began existing without exercise. The forced stillness helped me begin to discover that I was worthy without exercise.

When I first began exercising again I looked at the challenges I'd have to face and what eating disordered thoughts would surface. Before I even began introducing any physical activity back into my life, I had to anticipate how the eating disorder was going to react and use it as a way to sneak back in.

The first forms of exercise I engaged in were short walks around the neighborhood and yoga. I had to remain extremely mindful as I began exercising again. I had to stay present and notice when the eating disorder was encouraging me to make decisions based on weight, calories, or self-hatred.

Eventually, after many mindful walks, I was allowed to bring my bike to the Center to go for a bike ride. These measures, bringing a bike and going for a ride, were rarely allowed at the Center, but my therapists knew how important it would be for me to get back on my bike and have a safe place to return to in order to process the emotions that surfaced during the ride.

I rode six miles. For someone who was used to riding over 100 at once, it was torture to return to the Center having only done a tiny fraction of that. That morning, I ate oatmeal for breakfast, and was tempted to do the loop twice. I tried to release eating disordered thoughts from my mind as they surfaced. This meant recognising these thoughts as they surfaced and choosing to focus on other things. I noticed a fox. I saw beautiful houses. I saw other cyclists and tried to ignore the voice in my head growling, *I bet they're riding a lot further than me today!*

I resisted the urge to over-exercise and focused, instead, on the movement in my body. I began paying attention to how my body felt, and distracted myself by looking at colors and animals. In order to keep athletics in my life in a healthy fashion, I had to resist the eating disorder and all of the racing thoughts as I pedaled. I was gentle on my soul and began learning how to take care of my body through movement.

At the end of the ride I went back to the Center and processed the thoughts that surfaced. I thought that I hadn't done nearly enough, that I hadn't burned enough calories, that I wasn't skinny anymore and I needed to get my 'skinny body' back by exercising more.

Mindful walks, gentle yoga, and a six mile bike ride were the beginning of a new relationship with athletics for me. These were my avenues to redefine the role exercise played in my life.

I had to stop calling it "exercise". The word "exercise" is triggering. It indicates a chore that needs to be done in order for me to feel worthy. Iused to use "exercise" to abuse myself. Instead, I started referring to my athletics as "playtime." My exercise morphed into my playtime. The time I previously spent obsessing about calories, body shape, and weight loss, morphed into time spent thinking about the wind in my face, the sun on my skin, and the animals, trees, and landscapes I could look at. As I became more in tune with my breathing and listened to what my body needed, the eating disordered voices became easier to ignore. If I felt I needed to take it easy for a few days, I would. I'd always come back refreshed and ready for playtime.

Staying in tune with my body gave me renewed energy that made me feel like I was buzzing inside. I was outdoors playing and taking care of my body because it was fun and it was beautiful. I allowed myself to be healed out in nature, by the mountains and the fresh air. I was innocent, childlike, discovering how my body moves through space. The air on my skin, the sweat tickling my back. Instead of paying attention to weight and calories, I was paying attention to how my energy manifests in the world and in my body.

Playtime can be a place for me to escape, a place to reduce stress, but is not something I use against myself. I don't use it as a form of manipulation against myself to measure my worth, or prove that I'm not lazy. I don't use it to redeem myself, to earn my right to have fun, or earn my right to relax. I can use my playtime to help me stay in tune with my body's needs, to help me stay in tune with nature, to help me feel rejuvenated.

Playtime is not obligatory; it is movement, an exploratory activity. Instead of using athletics as a way to ignore my body, to prove something, to isolate, or punish myself, it is a way to ground myself and practice listening to my body. Instead of gaining outside approval, I began seeking internal well-being. In order to play as much as I do now, I have a pact with myself that I take care of my body first: I eat when I'm hungry, I sleep when I'm tired.

I CANNOT SEE THE OUTCOME OF THE JOURNEY, BUT I CAN TAKE THE NEXT STEP

Envisioning life without an eating disorder

At first I could not envision what my life would look like without an eating disorder. I didn't know what I would do in my spare time, what I would think about, or even how to develop relationships. My entire life had been so entwined in my eating disorder that I couldn't imagine my life without it. It had always been everything to me. I had no idea who I was without an eating disorder. It was my identity; it made all of my decisions and dictated every moment of my life.

My real life, my recovery life, was out there waiting for me and I had no clue what it would look like. I didn't know what my goals would be if I wasn't pursuing the ideal body. I didn't know what relationships would look like if I wasn't distracted by the pursuit of the ideal body. I didn't know what I would fill my time with, if not the pursuit of the ideal body. My eating disorder was my religion and I couldn't imagine what life would be like without the faith I always had in it.

To begin envisioning my life without an eating disorder, I started simply thinking of ways I could take better care of myself, my surroundings, and the people in my life. It was simple, I would focus on sleeping, eating enough, showering, brushing my teeth, and taking good care of myself. I had lost touch with taking care of my simple needs. First, I focused on self-care. Then I started looking to the outside world to see what other people did without eating disorders. Like Tarzan, learning to be human. These observations led me to stay in the moment and listen to people, have real relationships, have real conversations, and have experiences without the distraction of the eating disorder. I watched what others did, what others were capable of, and began to mimic their lives.

I started wanting to sort through all of my belongings, organize all my possessions, have a garage sale. I began wanting my life to be full of interactions with other people, experiences with other people. I wanted to make memories that had nothing to do with food, weight, or body image. I wanted to have instances in my life that were not related to how I feel about my body.

I started seeing myself with the energy to do all these things and the ability to pursue different goals. I began feeling a renewed energy, a renewed life, without my eating disorder. At first, I didn't believe this could happen to me- I just started believing it was a possibility for *other* people. I began listing all of the things I saw other people doing that I might want to do someday. As I made this list of experiences, I wanted to participate in them, no matter how mundane the activities seemed.

I began to tell myself, *"This is what my real life could look like."* And I began to believe it.

This included finding a place to live, meeting new people, going to farmer's markets, taking classes on random subjects. I could go to community events and concerts. I could read books. I could sleep in, wake up, kiss my boyfriend, read a book, drink some coffee, and not feel guilty about existing. I could get out of my comfort zone and explore the world.

The first time I remember feeling like these experiences were a possibility for me was a day in treatment when eating breakfast seemed normal. We were all in good places in our recovery, we were behaving like women without eating disorders, like a group of friends hanging out on a Saturday morning. We were able to hold a great conversation over muffins and not agonise over every bite. We spent the afternoon discussing a floor plan and then reorganizing the furniture. We went for a drive, looking for garage sales, and gawking at pretty houses. The day was ruled by moment to moment spontaneity. This special Saturday was not driven by obsessions with food, or thoughts about what we ate or had to eat later. We did whatever we felt like doing. We held great conversations throughout the day about body piercings, jobs, tattoos, school, boyfriends, and other things that our lives consisted of. These weren't just superficial conversations to distract us from our obsessions with food and body image. They were real conversations about our lives away from CHS. We were able to internalize that we could have, and participate in lives without eating disorders. Doing laundry, organizing furniture, and doing arts and crafts seem like simple, negligible things, but it was the first day I felt normal. I went to bed believing that I could live my life without an eating disorder.

From there, I began thinking about how I wanted my relationships to look and play out in my life. I was able to begin forming goals that I actually believed I could accomplish. I began believing my life could take shape without the help of an eating disorder. I wanted my friendships to be true bonds of trust, not competitions. I would not spend my time comparing myself to other people. I began believing I could have relationships that could enrich my soul. I would experience people in ways my eating disorder never let me. I began believing that my body is a vessel for life and love. My body would take me on adventures; my body would be there to experience life with me, not to be a punching bag. I would stop trying to escape from my body. My mind, body, and soul would act as one, instead of trying to control each other.

I would be able to remember things. I would make memories. I would be fully present in moments. I would remember more than what pant size I was wearing that day. I would remember more than how thin I felt or what mood I was in based on the perception of my body that day. I gave myself permission to experience life. I gave myself unconditional permission to fail at anything and everything. Because I started to believe I didn't have to be perfect all the time. I would find the energy to accomplish anything I wanted to. This was all very exciting to me. I began wanting my life to be in balance to take on life's challenges. I wanted to learn, teach, and experience. This is what my life would look like without an eating disorder.

BEAUTY COMES IN ALL SHAPES AND SIZES

Disentangling Distorted Body Image

While disentangling the many aspects of my eating disorder, I found that body image is the piece that links everything together. 'Body image' is how one perceives their body, whether it is based in reality or not. It is one's internal representation of their body. It can be accurate, but more commonly is a distorted, negative product of the imagination. I began to sort through every aspect of my body image. In order to disentangle myself from my body hatred, I did endless activities to delve deeper and attempt to uncover the roots of my distorted body image.

The body hatred associated with my eating disorder was so severe it was blinding. It would take over everything, every thought in my mind. I had tunnel vision when it came to my body perception. Frequently, it was all I could focus on. If I felt "fat" on a certain day, it felt like the end of the world to me. I would do anything, go to any lengths, including self-harm, to change it. When suffering from an eating disorder, nothing compares to the shame of feeling fat. The eating disorder would have me dispising my body so much, I wanted to tear myself out of my skin. I wanted to rip my hair out. I wanted to cut my fat off. I would do anything to change how my body looked on any given day.

Having this severe body hatred is one of the most torturing aspects of the eating disorder. It made me loathe going out in public for fear I wouldn't fit anywhere or that I would be the focus of hatred and ridicule. I was terrified of prejudice and people mistreating me for being fat. I was scared of being made fun of. It made me feel like I didn't belong or I didn't even deserve to exist in the world. I was depressed going in and out of every day hating my body so much I could barely get out of bed.

With eating disorders, body image issues are usually the first to surface and the last to go. It is the only struggle I continue to have after over 10 years in recovery. Because I placed so much importance on my appearance and size of my body, it was all encompassing. Being, feeling, or appearing "fat" was the end of the world to me. Some days I thought I would have rather died than be as fat as I thought I was. I felt guilty that others had to look at my body. I felt like I didn't fit anywhere, I felt like my clothes were never going to fit, and if my jeans felt tight, I deserved nothing- or severe punishment. I didn't deserve to exist. If I was having a fat day, I deserved nothing.

The way I perceive my body feels so real and changes from minute to minute. If something stressful happens, suddenly my body swells up and I feel as though I've gained 20lbs in five minutes. If something stressful happens with my family, or my friends, or boyfriend, or finances, or if I make a mistake, my eating disorder suddenly has me seeing, and feeling, my body as many sizes bigger than I actually am. It has me going to great lengths to try to change the size of my body.

It has taken a lot of time to separate myself out from this image. Initially I had to realize, and fully understand, that my body will not gain 20 lbs overnight or in a matter of minutes. The way I perceive my body is directly related to my emotional state.

Distorted body image is also a coping mechanism to escape from a current situation. If I can think about my fat body, how fat I am, and how I'm going to change it, I don't have to think about the current stressful situation. It is self-hatred portrayed through the eating disorder's voice.

"*If you weren't so fat, none of this would be happening to you. You'd have a solution. Skinny people do not have these problems.*"

I, once again, had to try to separate myself out from the voice of the eating disorder. I had to begin to see that I was a healthy weight, and that if I was seeing my body as overweight, or fat, this had come through the filter of the eating disorder and was incorrect. I had to continue to tell myself that going to any lengths to try to change the shape of my body would be harmful and in vain.

Once I realized that this was just my eating disorder playing tricks with my imagination, I began to identify body image thoughts as those of the eating disorder. I started by looking at my body rituals. I was, once again, baffled that I was not the only person who engaged in these behaviors. Body rituals are so common with eating disorders that there is a name for it. I thought I was the only person who had various, compulsive, behaviors to keep track of my body size. I was finally surrounded by others who did the exact same thing, all day, everyday.

As someone who's hated their body for so long I had a long list of rituals I did to gauge my body size and therefore, inventory my self-worth for the day. These rituals let the eating disorder determine if I was fat or skinny that day. I would inventory if I was pretty and thin, or fat and ugly. Some of the compulsive body ritual behaviors included:

- Are my elbows larger than my arms?
- Can I see and grab onto my collar bones?
- Can I take my pants off without unbuttoning them?
- Checking the size of my stomach compared to the size of my breasts
- Do my jeans feel tight?
- Can I see my ribcage? Can I see it in my back?
- How big is the space between my thighs?
- Can I see the tendons in the back of my knees?

Once, while in treatment, I was sitting in the living room. I had a rubber bracelet on my ankle. I had worn it proudly as an anklet for a few months, since it was the perfect size for my wrist-sized ankle. It was a LiveStrong bracelet, so there was no mistaking the type of jewelry it was and where it should be worn. The RA looked at me and said sternly, "Put that on your wrist where it belongs." My eating disorder immediately became confrontational at the thought of abolishing one of my body rituals, one of the ways it kept track of my size.

"Whhhyyyy?" I whined, like a whiny, rebellious teenager.

"You know exactly why. Wear it on your wrist or don't wear it at all."

At the time, I thought the RA's were being mean and demeaning. But when I took that bracelet off of my ankle, I eliminated a body ritual, and I took power away from the eating disorder.

Each eating disorder has different daily rituals to keep the victim in it's grips; to check body size, to compare today's size to yesterday, and set goals for tomorrow. These are performed daily, habitually, ritualistically (often countless times a day) and are a way to continually obsess about the body. The behaviors listed above are examples of just a few in the litany of body rituals, or body-checks, I'd do daily to abuse myself in order to stay thin. Whatever my eating disorder found while performing these body checks was not based in reality. When there was a beautiful, healthy body in front of my eating disorder's eyes, it found every flaw. It invented flaws where there were none and forced me to try to change my body. These obsessive behaviors of taking inventory of my body had me believing that I was much larger than in actuality.

I'd spent 20+ years developing body checking habits, so it was extremely difficult to put an end to these behaviors. Body checking, gauging my size in mirrors and windows, was a huge piece of my everyday life. Body rituals were an 'all day-everyday' behavior that I engaged in with my eating disorder. While in treatment, and the years following treatment, I made a conscious effort to stop doing these checks, or at least notice when I was doing them. I also made an effort to stop compulsively looking in mirrors and windows as I passed by. I began to break the habit a little piece at a time. I started recognising when I was body checking. I recognized without judgement. I couldn't stop entirely, but I at least started to notice when I was looking in windows to check the size of my stomach. I simply started by noticing when I was doing it. Noticing without judgement. It was very important that I didn't judge myself for body checking, I just noticed when I was doing it.

"I'm looking at the size of my legs again," I'd think, and then I'd give myself permission to stop. I'd give myself permission to not be affected by what I saw while looking at my legs.

I stopped trying to take my pants off with the buttons and zipper still closed. I stopped wearing bracelets as anklets. Each of these rituals was a way for the eating disorder to keep track of my body size, and keep a hold on me. I stopped body-checking to get validation for myself, and instead became curious about why the behaviors were there and what role these behaviors played in my life.

While in the grasps of the eating disorder, I body checked for personal validation. By judging my body, I knew how to treat, and think about, myself. Fifteen years of body-checking served as fuel for the eating disordered thoughts and behaviors, but was no longer serving me in my recovery. I took dry erase markers and wrote positive affirmations on the mirrors in the bathrooms. Everytime I went to look at, and hate, my body, there was something nice to read instead.

After many months and conscious effort, the urge to engage in rituals that I'd been performing since I was a child lessened. These habits have never fully gone away, but I refuse to do anything with the information that filters into my brain as a result of these impulsive checks. I've accepted that I still body-check to a certain degree, but I am very aware that it is happening and I do not let eating disordered thoughts enter my brain. I've worked hard combating the urges and not letting the eating disorder invade my mind with distorted body image and lead me into self-destructive behaviors.

Another way I began combating my body image issues was entertaining the idea that negative qualities are not attached to the way my body looks or moves. I started realizing that the body I see everyday is different than the body the rest of the world sees. I had to try to care less about what others thought of my body. That I see myself, and perceive myself as much bigger than the rest of the world sees me. It's as if I have a magnifying glass on every perceived flaw, every imperfection, every non-existent bulge. I see my body as many disconnected parts: stomach separate from hips and legs, shoulders separate from arms. Instead of the pieces making up a functional, whole body, I see every piece making up a body much larger than I desire.

To continue to disentangle my body hatred, I began thinking about my body's function. I thought of every part of my body I wanted to change. Instead of hating these pieces, I began focusing on their function and contribution to my life. I stopped focusing on imperfections. I told myself that my stomach digests the food that gives me energy. My energy helps me think. My legs help me ride bikes. My arms are the source of my art and creativity. This helped me begin to accept the body that I'm in.

Moving my focus to the function of my body was only the first step in a very long process of body acceptance. I began observing my body and trying not to judge it. I simply tried to observe what was there: legs, arms, face, tummy, shoulders. These parts of my body are parts of me and I am not willing to make sacrifices to change them. This is the body I am in. In the same way I cannot change my height or my foot size, I began accepting that I have a natural body size if I stop trying to alter it. I began accepting the natural state of my body when not under siege from the eating disorder.

One of my Goals while in treatment was to do a mental body-scan. A simple, basic, elementary body-scan. I was supposed to close my eyes and check-in with different parts of my body. I was supposed to note how each piece felt, acknowledge its presence, and accept what my body was telling me. I was supposed to do this everyday without judging my body. I was supposed to start at my toes, feel my toes, see how they felt as part of my body. From there I move up to my ankles, then my calves. Having a background in theatre I was overly familiar with the body-scan. But this time it was different. I could never make it past my knees. So I would try to scan from my head down. Head, eyebrows, eyes, ears, neck, shoulders, and that is where my body disappeared.

It was as though I had no body between my shoulder and my knees. I couldn't access it, couldn't connect to it, couldn't acknowledge it's presence. I didn't want to check-in with the body that existed between my shoulders and my knees. I didn't want the body that was there. My thighs and my torso are the parts of my body I judge the most severely and I could not acknowledge them without judgement. I spent hours in meditation trying to find my stomach and thighs in my mind.

For years, this was difficult, but I continued to try to check-in and acknowledge my body without judgement. Simple actions, like putting lotion on, helped me begin to feel my body in areas I chose to ignore in the past. Or breathing gratitude into my legs or digestive system, helped me get in touch with these body parts I had previously despised.

While I was in treatment, I had a chance to wander around an art gallery for a few minutes. I saw a few sculptures. Nudes. I saw curvaceous figures of women. I thought it was beautiful artwork. These figures were dancing, full of life, full of love. There were figures of men and women wrapped around each other. They were beautiful, frolicking figures. Completely alive. I came to the realization that if someone were to do a sculpture of me, at my goal weight, the weight at which I entered the Center, the weight I had tried my whole life to be, it would not produce a sculpture full of joy, love or frolicking. It would look terribly sad and destitute. It would be a child-like figure, starving, cold, and empty, with nothing to give the world. No energy for dancing, no love, just sadness. I realized then that I wanted to be seen as full of life and love, not shivering, lifeless depression. I wanted others to gaze on me as I did those life-filled sculptures. I wanted to be a lovely, dancing sculpture.

My self worth
is not determined by a number on a scale

The Burning & Bashing Ceremony

In recovery, I missed weighing myself. I missed the numbers. I missed having a number to attach to myself. I missed defining myself by the number on my scale.

One of my Goals was to do a Creative Representation of my scale, what it meant to me, and it's significant in my life. I drew it as a corset, and a bodice, with the scale numbers across the chest and someone's hands pulling tightly on the strings around the waist. This was exceptionally meaningful for me, as I love getting dressed up in costumes and corsets. And I loved my scale. The hands were those of my eating disorder, always pulling tighter on the corset strings, always in control.

My relationship with my scale was a huge piece of my eating disorder. I desperately wanted to weigh myself, all the time. My scale, and the number it gave me, meant everything to me. It was how I knew how to treat myself each day. If the number was too high, I would restrict more and strive for a lower number. If the number was lower than I expected, I'd see how much lower I could get it. I was deeply emotionally attached to my scale and the number attached to my body. I would play games with my scale, and let it dictate exactly how I felt each day. I felt it gave me concrete goals I could achieve when I weighed myself countless times a day. Most times, nothing else in my life mattered, because I knew that number and it made me feel like I was in control.

I loved the way the number dropped before I came to the Center. It just kept dropping. The dial would spin and land on a number my formerly "fat" self would never believe possible. I would see that number in neon lights in my head all day. I'd go back to double check to see if it was real. I remember thinking, "if this number is real, what else is possible?"

Could the number in neon lights be lower tomorrow? No matter what happened during the day, no matter what anyone would say to me, anything could happen, and that number would flash before my eyes.

Oh yeah? Well ___ lbs lost, and counting. What've you got?

My scale, and the number it gave me, was my answer to everything.

I missed not being able to weigh myself. I missed it so much I had dreams about it. I thought my scale defined who I was, it was my identity. I relied on that number. I didn't have to have a personality, because I had a number. Without my scale, I felt like I was just wandering around, aimlessly trying to define myself, not knowing where to begin.

I remember the day in treatment when I went to put on my skinny jeans and they didn't fit. I was immediately reminded of the first day they did fit, back when I was pursuing the ideal body. I clearly remember the day they did not fit anymore and I had to go up a jean size. I tried to keep a good attitude, to ignore it, to keep my chin up all day. I had been working hard to eat my meals, and listen to and honor my hunger signals. I was self portioning at that point- meaning I was responsible for listening to my hunger signals, portioning out my own food, and eating what I felt was appropriate.

But that night at dinner, I couldn't bring myself to eat. I could barely eat at all. I just sat there crying. Crying over what I thought was my new fat body. I missed being on the road to skinny. I had sacrificed so much for my body, to fit into my skinny jeans. I had given up everything, and I felt like it was all ruined. I loved those jeans and what I thought they told the world about me.

As soon as the post-dinner discussion was over, I went upstairs and changed out of the triggering clothing I was wearing. I put yoga pants on and went back downstairs.

I did not want to accept that my body was changing, but it was. This was the moment I had feared. I knew it was going to happen eventually. I knew that I couldn't healthy maintain the weight I had previously been at.

I had been in treatment for seven weeks at that point and was really working on my body image. I was slowly learning that I needed to accept my natural body weight- whatever it may be. I needed to stop trying to manipulate it and allow my body to level out naturally.

I didn't know where my body weight was going to end up and that terrified me. I had to trust that if I was eating when I was hungry and stopping when I was full, my body size and shape would end up exactly where it was supposed to.

I was in the process of re-creating a picture of myself in my mind. I was trying to convince myself that I wasn't the chubby girl I once thought I was. I was beginning to believe that I could be a beautiful woman, in a woman's body, wearing women's clothing, glowing with life. Beginning to believe that I could have healthy hair, a healthy attitude, and a healthy mind.

But this act, abandoning the pursuit of the ideal body, was an act of faith. It was surrendering and giving up something I had invested my whole life in controlling. I had to surrender to the process of recovery. I had to trust the dietician and the Center. No one told me how much courage it was going to take. It was as though I was giving up a religion. I was giving up a belief system. I had spent my life trying to be thin and, suddenly, not having that focus, giving it up, was heart wrenching. The way I kept control of my weight was the one piece of myself that I felt kept me in control. It made me unique, it made me different from other people.

Now that my skinny jeans didn't fit, I could no longer identify with that piece of me, I had to let it go. I was no longer the "skinny girl" . When I stopped identifying myself by my weight, I felt I had nothing. My whole life, I had held the desire to be thin deep in my heart. I held it close to my heart, like I would a baby. I remember telling my therapist that thinking about my eating disorder brings me comfort. When I'm engaging in the behaviors it feels like I'm cradling and soothing a baby. It's mine and no one else's. It's warm and comfortable. Like a best friend, it's loyal, always there for me. Now that I was starting to let these beliefs go, I had no idea what to expect.

No one told me it was going to take that much courage to recover from an eating disorder. Every day, I woke up and faced new fears. Every morning, I strapped my armor on, gathered my courage, and got ready to fight. Every night I had nightmares that my clothes didn't fit, that no clothes would ever fit, or had binged and not purged. Everyday was a battle to discover new aspects of the eating disorder, their roots, and destroy them. Every second of every day was exhausting, fighting my way out, trying to silence the voices in my head. I continued to remind myself that the eating disorder wreaks havoc on me. I had to remember that it is not a gentle loving friend, but a tyrannical beast trying to kill me.

I was always dying to be thin. There was always a part of me that believed that if I'd died, I won. If I died, I was the most successful in my eating disorder. I was so good at it, it actually killed me. "Congratulations, you starved yourself to death, you no longer have to be in your body. You are the best. You are perfect. Rest in peace."

I had to challenge myself to see it in a different light, and began to analyze what the eating disorder took away from me. I began to question if it was ever worth the body it got me. It was never worth it. The eating disorder took so much away from me. It was never worth all the sacrifices I made to get the body. I kept reminding myself that a life was waiting for me, a life outside of this living hell. I reminded myself everyday what I was fighting for. I kept jumping into the unknown, letting go of that child, the friend, the baby I kept so close to my heart.

The morning after I grew out of my skinny jeans, I went into the bathroom, and the RA's had made a sign that said, "Good Morning, Beautiful Bri. It's going to be a beautiful day." That sign hung in my bathroom for years after my treatment. It reminded me that everyday is a new battle. That I fought yesterday and I can fight again. Even if it was just for a moment, just for a second, those were seconds that went by when I was not hating my body. I put on jeans that fit and went downstairs for breakfast. I hated it, but I was beginning to accept that my body has nothing to do with my personality. It would take time to truly accept my body, to truly believe that I am an amazing person regardless of the number on my jeans. It's taken years of going through the motions; putting clothes on that fit, not checking in the mirror, and not stepping on a scale, for me to accept my body as it is. I have become completely unwilling to change my body.

While in the grips of an eating disorder, every piece of clothing has an emotional connection, which makes it very important to have clothes that fit properly and are comfortable. If my clothes don't fit, I'll be tempted to change the size of my body to fit into them. If I have jeans that are too small and think I'll fit in them "someday", I know I need to get rid of them. Keeping those jeans would be allowing myself to be haunted by the pursuit of the ideal body. It is healthier for me to get rid of the temptations that lead me to constantly want to change my body. I need to buy clothes that fit my natural body- the body I exist in without dieting or manipulation of my weight- the body I have without an eating disorder.

At this point in my treatment, my therapists decided I needed new clothes, not the clothing I adorned myself in while in the grips of my eating disorder. Of course this was a good opportunity to practice shopping for clothes that fit. So, my therapist took me out for an afternoon on the town: we went shopping for jeans and then went out to lunch. Both equally different outings, squashed into one afternoon.

I was tortured buying new clothes. I hated trying them on, I hated the mirrors, the lighting, the numbers. I used to go to thrift stores, buying a couple things for cheap and then trying them on at home. If the clothes don't fit, I re-donate them back to the thrift store, no big deal. Trying on clothes used to be tedious because I always grab clothes off the rack that are too big- as I genuinely see my body much larger than it is and that clothing two sizes too big will fit. When I put on clothes that are way too big, the eating disorder congratulates me for a second before telling me to become even thinner. If I grab a smaller size, I am terrified it won't fit. I am devastated if it doesn't fit, if it is too small. This process forces me to want to change the size of my body to fit into the smaller clothing. I can never win. I needed to experience buying a new pair of jeans in the company of a therapist so I could process all of these emotions and thoughts as we went.

We went to JC Penny and searched through the racks. I picked out a pair of sparkle-butt jeans that fit great and were incredibly comfortable. In order to remain recovery oriented, I had to detach my emotions from the size, detach from the number. It took a ton of focus, and commitment to my recovery, to stay in the moment and accept the number for what it was. It is a number on a piece of fabric, printed by some company so it's easier for customers to find one that fits. It says nothing about who I am as a person, what I do, or what I can accomplish. It is just a number. This number is not my happiness. It does not make me imperfect or less capable than anyone else. I can still accomplish my dreams, I am still worthy, no matter what number is on my jeans.

All of these thoughts raced through my head as I purchased my new jeans. They were beautiful and apparently looked good on me. I left the store hopeful that I'd see it someday.

We then proceeded to lunch. It was getting somewhat easier to eat in restaurants, as we went out to lunch every Wednesday. The challenges with eating in public were numerous and endless. The biggest challenge for me was thinking that everyone was watching me eat. Which was mortifying for me, because I wanted to classify myself as a non-eater, someone who never got hungry and never ate. For most of my life, eating in public was traumatic. To complicate it, I was terrified of the food served in restaurants. I was afraid of the portions and having all that food sitting in front of me made me feel like a pig- even if I wasn't eating it. If I did eat it, it usually tasted so good I would start to wonder what they put in it to make it so flavorful. I would begin to think about the butter and the cheeses, the fat content, and the caloric count. I would also feel like I was indulging in something I didn't deserve, something that made me gluttonous.

Another fear I had was that if I did begin to eat, I wouldn't be able to stop and I'd have to go throw it all up afterward. Throwing up was no longer an option. Our bathroom visits were monitored, so I would be stuck with all of that food inside me, piling up in pockets of fat. Eating out was always rough because all of these thoughts were racing through my head, creating a paralyzing anxiety. I would get such severe anxiety in restaurants, that my vision would go blurry while trying to read the menu, which made it impossible to read or make decisions. To be proactive about my recovery, I used to look at the menus online before going out, so I could make my decisions ahead of time. This made it so I already knew, going into the situation, what to order. This is how I dealt with my anxiety, so it wouldn't take over and make it impossible for me to operate in restaurants.

We went to a cute vegetarian restaurant upstairs from a coffee house and ordered quesadillas with homemade salsa. It was like I was out with a friend, not a therapist. The kitchen was visible from our table and she mentioned that the waiter kept, "checking me out." I giggled and shrugged it off. At the end of our meal we decided to get cookies for a dessert. This was a huge hurdle for me, eating sweets, or dessert foods, for no reason except to enjoy it. I was starting to believe in the empowerment of a woman sitting at a table enjoying a dessert on her own, or with company, for no reason except that she wants to enjoy the hell out of it. So, I gathered my courage, calmed my nerves, ignored the voices in my head telling me that I'm not allowed to eat cookies, and went over to a small fridge where the cookies were displayed. In my life up until treatment, my eating disorder would have never allowed me to look at dessert after the meal with the intention of eating it. That day, I held my head high, and picked out cookies for us to enjoy.

The waiter who had been making eyes at me earlier got a cute grin on his face and said, "Looking for something sweet?"

"Always," I said as I turned casually to him, smiled, and then walked back to our table.

My eating disorder was screaming at me, that I should be ashamed of myself, that I'm not one of them, that I don't eat sweets as we enjoyed our cookies and giggled about the waiter.

That was one of the first distinct times I remember actively standing up to my eating disorder in public, where there was a lot of stimulus, many opportunities and reasons to give in and let the eating disorder take hold. I didn't let old habits creep back in. I made a recovery oriented decision and took action. I felt liberated. The cute waiter, and the other people in the restaurant didn't think I was fat, gluttonous, or gross for eating a cookie. He probably appreciated my attitude and gesture. He probably appreciated the care-free, relaxed nature in which I responded. I've been able to replicate that attitude in stressful times, remembering my 'win' that afternoon.

After buying new jeans and making the creative representation of my scale, my treatment team and I decided it was time to rid myself of obvious triggers- my old clothes and my scale. They helped me host a Burning and Bashing ceremony to part with these sacred items. The items my eating disorder used to keep me as a prisoner.

On Sept 19, three months after entering treatment, we lit a fire in the firepit in the backyard, took a huge bag of my "skinny clothing", and headed out back. Each of my house mates got a piece of clothing and a sharpie marker. We cut up the clothes into pieces and decorated them with affirmations- positive affirmations about recovery and body image.

Some of the residents wrote about what their lives would look like without eating disorders. I kept a few pieces of clothing whole, a few articles I wanted to watch ignite in one piece.

We proclaimed the affirmations and threw the fragments of clothing into the fire. I burned jeans, shirts, and running shorts. Childrens shorts, that no adult should be able to wear, that I sacrificed my life to fit into, ignited quickly as I cried. I sobbed. I was attached to these clothes with every ounce of my being. These articles told me who I was everyday and I'd been so proud to fit into them.

I blew my nose into a summer dress, a dress that made me feel like a precious doll when I wore it, and threw it into the flames. The day I wore that summer dress was the day everyone knew how sick I was. That was the day people stopped addressing me about my weight and started addressing my roommate and my teachers. That was the point when those around me knew I had a 'problem' and had no idea what to say anymore. They had run out of questions to ask and words of comfort to offer. They started going behind my back, they knew I wasn't listening to their concerned voices, that I was past any help they could offer. That was the day the probing questions were silenced by my painfully thin body parading around in that summer dress.

I held my head high as it burned, knowing it couldn't plague me anymore.

It took about an hour to burn all of the clothing. Watching denim burn was the most difficult, most empowering thing I had ever done. Denim turns bright magenta before it turns to flame. It was beautiful.

It took a lot of courage to burn one specific pair of jeans. I never thought I'd have the courage to get rid of those jeans. I held onto them, gripped them, hesitated, and heaved huge sighs of grief, and relief as I watched them go up in flames.

As the flames danced before me, I thought of everything I had done to fit into those clothes. I had sacrificed everything and had been so proud when they fit. I remembered how they told me everyday how I was doing- either I was a good, skinny girl if they fit, or I was reprimanded if they felt tight. The grief for the loss of my eating disorder struck me deep, but was quickly replaced with relief that I would *never have to fit in those clothes again!*

While the clothes were still smoldering, we made our way out to the driveway with my scale that had been locked up with other contraband. I grabbed a boom box and a sledge hammer, and set my beloved scale down on the pavement. If someone had asked me, even a month before, to smash my scale, I would've cried out in agony, "DON'T DO IT!" But I had come a long way in my recovery process and was ready for the next step. I pressed play on the boom box and my recovery theme-song began playing.

It was a pop song that came on the radio every time we'd gotten in the car that summer. *Battlefield* by Jordan Sparks lulled me away as I said goodbye to my scale.

Don't try to explain your mind, I know what's happening here,
One minute it's love and then it's like a battlefield,

My housemates stood on the porch, silently supporting me as I held my scale close to my heart. I caressed it, cried, set it down and backed away.

One word turns into a-
Why is it the smallest things that tear us down?
My world's nothing when you're gone,
I'm left here without a shield,
Can't go back now...

I thought about every time I stepped on that scale. Everything it had given me. Everything I'd done to please it. Every time I'd been proud. Every time I'd been devastated.

Both hands tied behind my back, for nothing,
These times when we climb so fast to fall again,

I sobbed. That scale had kept me like a prisoner, but it was my best friend.

I never meant to start a war,
You know I never wanna hurt you,
Don't even know what we're fighting for,
Why does love always feel like a battlefield?

I went back over, picked it up, looked at it longingly. I was sobbing so hard, I could barely breathe.

Can't swallow our pride, neither of us wanna raise that flag,
If we can't surrender we're both gonna lose what we had,
Both hands tied behind my back for nothing,
These times when we climb so fast to fall again,

I held the scale and thanked it for being in my life.

I never meant to start a war,
You know I never wanna hurt you.

Set it back down.

Don't even know what we're fighting for.

Out of pure habit, I zeroed it out.

Why does love always feel like a battlefield?

I couldn't see through the tears. I backed away once more and raised the hammer high above my head.

I guess you better go and get your armor,

I slammed the sledge hammer down on the scale as hard as I could. It shattered the front of the scale as I let out a scream and brought the hammer down again and again, screaming and crying. It was as though every piece of me that was ruined by my eating disorder took a swing at that scale. I was finally strong enough to retaliate. It was as though the soul that had been trapped within that scale was escaping with every swing of that hammer. I was escaping from that scale. After another minute of smashing and crying, I went limp and stood there crying as the song faded out.

I never meant to start a war,
You know I never wanna hurt you,
Don't even know what we're fighting for,
Why does love always feel like a battlefield?
I guess you better go and get your armor.

My housemates were cheering wildly from the porch, they were proud. I was proud and relieved. And exhausted. I have not, and will not, step on a scale to this day.

The physical acts, the physical battles, were tangible and necessary aspects of my recovery. I got rid of clothing that I would never be able to fit into again. I got rid of my scale that I should never step on again. I still have no idea what I weigh. I never step on scales. Ever. I attribute this success to the power I discovered in myself while I was smashing my scale. The freedom was tangible. I knew I'd been a prisoner for years and the only way to keep my freedom is to stay off of scales.

I know and understand that I will probably never be able to know my weight. At first, if I was having a rough day, I would even avoid walking down or near aisles at the store that displayed scales, so as not to be tempted to weigh myself. I know that having the knowledge of that number will ruin me and my health. It sounds overdramatic, but I know I have worked too hard to even slightly risk my recovery.

I do not even get weighed at the doctor's office. When I mention this most people say, "You can just turn around, you won't even see the number." My response is always the same, "If that number is written down somewhere, I will find it. Even if by accident. It is not worth the risk." The sound of the scale, the numbers clanking, the feeling of it under my feet, everything about getting weighed is triggering to me. And I do not trust anyone else with that number. The nurses, the admin, weven the doctors don't understand how hard I have worked for my recovery and I will not risk it.

I have unfortunately been in many confrontations at the doctor's office because of this. I have been called a bitch by nurses, and I'd rather be name-called by a medical professional than know my weight. After one of the more aggressive encounters, I talked to a doctor who has a very long history with my family. She was the doctor who told my mom when she was pregnant with me and she was the doctor who did my physical before getting admitted to CHS. She was able to go into my patient file and write "Do Not Weigh" in my file. In addition, she gave me the verbiage of how to refuse the scale in the doctor's office. I say, "Can we skip the scale today?" The nurses usually agree. If they get aggressive, I say, "It should say in my file Do Not Weigh Patient." This has worked for me every single visit for over 10 years. In case these two phrases do not deescalate the situation, my doctor told me to "refuse the procedure." For some people in recovery, this may be a bit overdramatic, but this is my boundary that I am not willing to bend for anyone. I stick to it no matter what.

I have no idea what I weigh and I will not seek out the knowledge of my weight because I know it will ruin me. I have no problem going my whole life not knowing my weight. I get to develop my personality based on who I am, not based on what the scale tells me. I get to develop a life based on experiences, making memories, friends, family, and fun. My life is no longer measured in calories or BMI.

Through the Burning and Bashing Ceremony, I realized my strength and found my freedom. My refusal to know my weight has been an integral part of my success in my recovery.

I AM NATURALLY BEAUTIFUL WHEN I AM MYSELF

Fat Vs Thin

The next thing I had to do was look at why I wanted to be skinny. Why did I desire thinness? I examined what "thin" meant to me. I examined every aspect of it. And I looked deep into what "fat" meant to me as well.

I first looked at my fears. I looked deep into my fear of eating and my fear of being fat. I thought it was a representation of greed or gluttony. I didn't want people to think I was spoiled or indulgent. When eating, I felt I was taking more than I deserve, that I was a gluttonous pig- only caring about myself. While eating, I felt I was drawing attention to myself and indulging in something I hadn't earned. I believed that eating was gluttonous. I believed that people who ate were fat, lazy, out of control, taking more than they need just because they can, and putting their needs before others. My fear was that when I ate, people would think that I can't control my needs or that I don't know how to take care of myself properly. I didn't want to be seen as needy, or more needy than those around me.

I also believed that when I ate, I would be perceived as frenetic. I didn't ever want to seem frenetic or out of control. I wanted to slide by, under the radar, and only be noticed for being the good girl who isn't needy, who doesn't want or need anything, the girl who is simply perfect. The girl who isn't going around frantically searching for ways to satisfy her needs.

I discovered that I wanted to be skinny because my mother was afraid of me being the opposite of skinny. Being real. Not being perfect. As daughters we absorb our mother's fears. We emulate and adopt their likes, dislikes, prejudices, and loves. She was afraid of me just being me. She wasn't afraid of me not being skinny. She wasn't afraid of me being fat. Her fear was of me being real. Being real would mean having needs, having a big personality. Her fear was that she didn't know what I was going to act like, it was a fear of the unknown. The fear of fat, the fear of loss of control, was a fear of the unknown.

It is important for me to see that much of my anxiety surrounding body weight originally stemmed from my mother's fear of being fat. My fear grew from hers. When my mother was young she was made fun of for being overweight and, unfortunately, that fear (whether she desired it to or not) got passed on to her children. It was passed down through her comments and actions, regardless of if she wanted it to or not. I always felt that a way to impress my mother was to lose weight, to be on a diet, or to be in shape and be fit.

I was a creative child. I was always doing ridiculous things, coming up with wild ideas (that hasn't changed) and my weight loss goals seemed like the only goals that were easy for my mother to support. So I set, and accomplished, weight loss goals to gain approval.

My fears of becoming fat developed early in my life. I grew up in a house that was extremely prejudiced against "fat people". I grew up listening to degrading comments that were directed at people who were overweight.

"That person really shouldn't be eating that."

Or, "Let's all be grateful," as we walked by an overweight person. We were supposed to be grateful that we were not overweight.

Disliking fat people and fearing weight gain became the norm. I had a membership to a gym by the time I was 10. My sister, my mom, and I were running 5ks together around the same time. Fitness was extremely important in our household.

Because I was so sensitive to comments directed at others, I would internalize, and misinterpret them, which led to self-doubt.

I would hear, "That person shouldn't be eating that." And immediately interpret it as, *If that person shouldn't be eating ice cream, maybe I shouldn't eat at all.*

Certain foods were absolutely not allowed in the house, unless it was a special occasion. I grew up fearing food. I was terrified of food clogging my arteries, making my blood pressure go up, and, most importantly, making me fat. Even though I didn't know what any of that meant. I also learned that over-eating, or eating when you're not hungry, will make you fat. I became fearful of eating when I wasn't hungry and began misinterpreting my hunger signals at a very young age.

My sister struggled with her hunger signals when we were young as well. At least my mom claimed that she did. My mom thought she had difficulty deciphering her hunger from sadness over our parents divorce and boredom. Her confusion, and living in a fat-fearing home, led me to not trust my hunger signals as well. I never trusted that my body was actually hungry, I thought I was just hungry because I was fat. To an adult (or someone without an eating disorder), this is illogical, but as a child that was the conclusion I drew. I believed that the hungrier I was, the fatter I'd get. I learned not to trust my hunger signals from a very young age. It took months in treatment to recognise and regain confidence in my hunger signals. It took practice to even admit that I was hungry. I eventually learned to honor my hunger by eating.

My fears surfaced once when I refused to put Cool Whip on a banana because I didn't want to be associated with the kinds of people who ate dessert. Dessert, in this case, was the Cool Whip. I explored why I didn't want to be associated with eating the Cool Whip. As I spoke with one of the therapists, I found that I associate people who eat dessert foods with being lazy, gluttonous, out of control, dirty, greedy, and, of course, fat. I did not want to be associated with that type of person. In my mind, eating the Cool Whip made me *one of them.* My eating disorder refused to let me eat desserts because I didn't want to be viewed as lazy, greedy, or gluttonous. But all the people in the room who I thought were beautiful, and whom I deeply respected, were eating the Cool Whip.

"You've been making the decision not to eat dessert and look where it's gotten you. You've been down that road. You are in a treatment facility. Why not try eating it? You don't know the outcome. You have two choices here: eat it or don't eat it. You already know the outcome of one choice. You've been that direction, you've been down that road. You get sick and miserable, your life falls apart. You've been there. Your other choice is to try it. Why not give it a try? You have no idea what awaits you if you just give it a try," my therapist said with an encouraging smile.

She was right. I had no idea what would happen if I ate desserts and 'dangerous foods'. All of the beautiful, strong, intelligent people in the room were eating the snack and I wasn't judging them for it. I was just grateful that I was the only strong one in the room refusing it. But I knew what it looked like when I refused to eat. I could no longer continue refusing food like I had been.

I, once again, put my faith in the process of recovery. One bite at a time, I ate the banana with the Cool Whip. No one assumed I was fat, lazy, or gluttonous for having eaten it. I just ate it. I did not gain 20lbs overnight, like I believed I would, from eating a dessert. My body used the food as fuel and burned it off just like any other food. I began applying this lesson to other aspects of eating and it proved useful in helping make the decision to eat. It helped me develop the skills to introduce 'dangerous' foods, foods that I was extremely fearful of, into my diet.

I was afraid of becoming fat, but being skinny wasn't everything I'd thought it would be. In fact, I didn't even know I was skinny; I still thought I was the chubby kid. I was proud of my weight loss, but I would have never labeled myself as skinny. The S-word. The word I tried my whole life to be, and failed miserably every time. Even when I had people grabbing my shoulders, telling me how skinny I was, that I was too thin, I scoffed because I wasn't thin *enough.* That there was no way I could be skinny. Skinny was a goal I would never accomplish. Skinny. If you say it enough times, it doesn't even sound like a word anymore. It means nothing but skin, nothing under your skin. It's a way of saying there's nothing to you. For so long, I was desperate to consist of nothing.

The allure of being skinny, of having nothing to me, was several fold. Along with being the center of attention, I didn't want to attract attention to myself, and my life, for fear of what I was doing wrong. If I could just be skinny enough, I would disappear off the radar. I would not have to accomplish anything and no one would judge my accomplishments. I wouldn't have to strive to be perfect anymore, I would just be perfect. I would be skinny. I would have something that no one else had. I would be unique in my body and everyone else would be envious.

My eating disorder was contradictory like this in many ways. It wanted me to be so thin I would disappear, yet, at the same time, it wanted me to be thin enough to get a ton of attention. I could never find the balance in my head.

I believed skinny people always got their way. I believed I'd be hired for more jobs, better liked, people would think I was stronger-willed, better behaved, tame, pure, untainted, strong, elegant. I thought being skinny would get me all of the attention I would ever need. I believed that being skinny would make me important and relevant, and that people would like me better. I believed that I would get more respect and be seen as perfect. I would be seen as in-control, smarter, and prettier if I were thin. Thin could always be thinner.

Taking the images and associations I had in my head of what it meant to be fat and what it meant to be skinny, I flipped my perspective. I did this as an exercise, an exploration for my recovery. I explored how my eating disorder was greedy and gluttonous and how my recovery would get me all of the things I thought being skinny would.

I was shocked to look at how greedy and gluttonous my eating disorder was. There's an excessive, insatiable desire to be thin. I was wasting myself and my personality to be thin. I only thought about food and exercise all the time, which was extremely selfish. I had no awareness of anything but my eating disorder and I pursued it frenetically. I cared only for my need to be thin, no one else's needs were taken into consideration. It wanted me to be the center of attention for all the wrong reasons. It made me wasteful with my time, with money, with food, and made me take advantage of people who loved and trusted me.

Looking at my eating disorder in this light made it slightly less appealing to me. Slowly the pieces began to untangle and unwind. The allure of the eating disorder began to dissipate. For years, my eating disorder had told me that when I ate I was the greedy, fat, gluttonous one. Now, looking at it with this perspective, it was the exact opposite. My eating disorder was forcing me to make greedy decisions, making me do gluttonous things.

The next step required me to look at all the qualities I associated with being thin and associate them with recovery instead. I began to see that being in recovery gives me all of the characteristics I associated with being thin. In a journal entry I wrote:

> "Staying in recovery brings my body and my soul back to its purest form. The form it was before I was tainted with bad body image and before I started hating myself. My eating disorder has wreaked havoc on my mind and on my body. Staying in recovery will keep me pure and striving toward the beautiful soul I was once in touch with. Staying in recovery will take a lot of strength because the eating disorder is so familiar to me. Going back to it and relying on it is the easy, the lazy, way out. It takes strength and a strong will to accept who I am. Staying in recovery will show that I am strong willed.

"My eating disorder is a 'pocket of insanity', it is an 'illusion of control', and is anything but tame inside my mind. When I can find true tranquility in my mind, within myself, without the eating disorder, that is what the world will see. True tranquility and strength. The true peace within me, freedom from the eating disorder, is true control, and is truly being well-behaved."

I began believing that 'well-behaved' means taking good care of my body. I began believing that my body and soul deserve respect and that being 'in control' means being true to myself. I used to believe that my eating disorder kept me in control, kept me strong, and by abusing myself I kept myself elegant. But having a strong recovery took much more energy and more strength. Relying on the eating disorder was lazy, the easy way out. Being strong, being brave, taking on challenges, and facing the unknown would take much more strength and elegance. Becoming elegant meant becoming truly elegant in my intentions toward my body, in my attitude toward my body, and my attitude towards others. I would be elegant in my actions. True elegance would be allowing myself to be pure in my acts of self-care. My inner-self could be tranquil and at peace. I would be pure and untainted, at peace. It would emanate outwards. I would be strong inside and out. I would be elegant in recovery.

I started to be gentle with myself and honor my needs. I could see myself for real, in all of my humanity. My ability to be loving and gentle with my true self is purity, strength, and elegance.

"I AM A WOMAN PHENOMENALLY, PHENOMENAL WOMAN, THAT'S ME"

- Maya Angelou

Feminine vs Masculine

I did not want to be in a woman's body. I never wanted to be in a feminine body. I believed society portrayed women as needy, clingy, and dependent. I felt women were portrayed as neurotic and control freaks. I felt that women were programmed to always be pleasing men and as soon as we had any needs of our own we were immediately labeled as a needy nuisance. I never wanted to be labeled or portrayed like this or associated with these traits; therefore, I didn't want to be in a woman's body. I thought it was embarrassing to be a female and carry the burden of being portrayed like this. I didn't want to be seen as being clingy or needy or embarrassing, so I refused to have any needs.

I realized at a young age that many traits that are socially acceptable when demonstrated by men are not as readily accepted when exhibited in a woman. I have always had a lot of natural energy and volume. I'm very determined and aggressive in pursuit of my goals. I used to think these traits were seen as overbearing when coming from a woman. I believed, subconsciously, that if I could be a boy, I would be more readily accepted. I felt like if I were in a boy's body, I wouldn't have to spend so much time proving myself, proving that I am not needy, high maintenance, or helpless just because I am in a woman's body. I thought that being a boy meant having unconditional permission to behave any way you wanted. After all, "Boys will be boys."

Being labeled as a 'tomboy', and distancing myself from my femininity, meant I could be loud, expressive, exploratory, athletic, and playful. Growing up as a "tomboy" gave me permission to forgo my femininity and become a boy. I felt like boys' behavior needed no excuses. I thought that boys could have opinions without being thought of as manipulative or bitchy.

When I wanted to detach from my feminine side, get out of my woman's body, my jaw would jut out and my hips would cease to sway when I walked. My defensive body language would project, "I can take care of myself, I am no damsel in distress." I noticed this would happen whenever I felt betrayed, hurt, or angry. I would want to escape from my body. I never wanted to appear weak, vulnerable, or typical. I felt the most vulnerable when experiencing emotions in a woman's body. I'd try to get out of this body, try to get away by ditching my femininity. When I felt emotions, a common defense mechanism for me would be to zone-out or rely on my masculine energy to carry me through my emotional experiences. I would cover up my emotional state, cover up my vulnerability, and show how tough I was.

Since a lot of this had to do processing emotions and trying to get out of my body, I began exploring how the eating disorder was connected and entangled with my desire to not be in a woman's body. In order to get in touch with my body and my emotions, I examined where all of these beliefs came from. I looked into why I wanted to escape from my body every time I felt emotional. I discovered that being in a woman's body made me feel vulnerable and open to ridicule.

Just noticing and articulating these past belief systems helped me learn to be vulnerable in my body and accept my emotional state- whatever it may be. I learned that experiencing emotions does not mean that I am crazy, hormonal, or needing to be avoided. Emotions indicated that I am a living being, in a woman's body that needed to be taken care of. I stopped trying to escape from my body as a defense mechanism. I began to accept that I could exist in my body, feeling whatever emotion I was feeling. As uncomfortable as these emotions can be, they are real and need to be acknowledged, not ignored. I learned that I do not need to lose weight and pretend to be in a curve-less, man's body to be acceptable.

This was all part of a journey to radically accept my body. I'm still on this journey. One of my assignments while in treatment was to write two letters: one from my mind to my body and one from my body to my mind. This powerful exercise helped me see the disconnect between the two. My mind was a tyrannical being; controlling and hating my body.

My body was desperate for an escape, desperate to just exist in peace. My mind was murdering my body. My body wished that my mind would listen and take proper care of it. My mind constantly wanted more from my body. Nothing was ever good enough, and my body was exhausted. My mind hated every aspect of my body and was actively trying to change it. The voice in my mind always told me that I didn't have needs-that if I had needs, I was a nuisance. I felt dirty when I had needs.

To begin healing the disconnect between the two, I began listening to and honoring my body's needs. Not just hunger, but I began learning how to take care of myself. For example, when I was tired, instead of allowing my mind to tell my body that it was weak and would never keep up, I'd take a nap. I began recognizing when my mind was expecting impossible things from my body. I began listening to my body instead of trying to control it. Instead of being embarrassed by my needs and squashing them, I began honoring them as they surfaced. When I was thirsty, I'd drink. When I was hungry, I would eat. These actions may seem simple, common sense even, to most, but I was accustomed to feeling inadequate and blaming all of my failures or shortcomings on my body's unrealistic needs.

With all of this knowledge and exploration, I began to heal the disconnect between my feminine and masculine, as well as between my mind and my body.

I LEARN MORE ABOUT MY INNER LIFE EVERY DAY

Discovering Hunger

I had to examine my hunger. I had to discover what hunger meant to me. I had to explore what I hunger for in my emotional life. I had to listen to the physical hunger in my body. My emotional hunger, my unmet emotional needs were reflected in how I viewed hunger in my body.

The women in my family hunger for acceptance, perfection, and image. The women in my family hunger for everyone on the outside to look in and see a perfect family. We hunger for approval. We want everyone to think we are the individuals doing everything right. We hunger for the proper answers. We yearn for what we are *supposed* to be doing. Growing up, it was unacceptable to hunger for anything more than an absolute basic need. It was acceptable to hunger for something to make you more successful, for example: more work. It was acceptable to hunger to be better.

My sister hungers to keep the peace, to have everything go over easy, without struggle. My sister's lack of appetite was evident. She never wanted anything out of turn, never craved or asked for much. She wanted peace. Our physical hunger was always brought into question. My sister's physical hunger was always questioned or unnecessary. My mother thought she was interpreting her emotions about our parent's divorce as hunger. Because she was a child, she wasn't allowed to trust her body. Her hunger was going to lead her to have to "watch her weight" for the rest of her life.

As a child, I drew the conclusion that if her physical hunger wasn't valid, or wasn't allowed, then mine should be brought into question as well. The condescending manner in which hunger was addressed made it seem as though if you were hungry, or getting food for yourself, that you were in trouble. Therefore, acknowledging hunger meant getting in trouble. If my sister expressed hunger, it would be met with the same tone of voice I would get for misbehaving.

Because of this, a thought-pattern developed in my head. I would have racing thoughts, "*If I go into the kitchen right now, will mom approve? Who will oppose me eating right now? Who will oppose how much I'm eating? Who will try to micromanage my meal for me?*" I saw this happen so often with my sister, that I became paranoid. I was paranoid of being in the kitchen without my mother granting me permission first. I was paranoid that my hunger wasn't real. I was paranoid that my hunger was just emotions. There was so much focus on my sister's hunger not being valid, that when I was hungry at the same time as my sister, or wanted the same food as her, I was paranoid that my own hunger wasn't valid. I needed permission to be hungry or to eat. I didn't want to let my mother down by actually feeling hunger. I couldn't possibly be feeling hunger. I didn't want to let my mother down by having the "mindless munchies."

I always felt bad for eating more than my mom on outings, in restaurants, and at family dinners. Looking back, I understand that I was an athletic, growing girl and needed to eat more than my mother. I couldn't figure out why I always felt gross and I always felt hungry. I would feel guilty for taking care of my hunger, because I felt that my hunger shouldn't be there in the first place. I made excuses for myself, special occasion excuses ("I'm having a growth spurt", "I worked really hard in PE today") so I could eat and take care of my appetite as a child.

Getting in touch with my hunger was extraordinarily challenging because my eating disorder, my guilt, my paranoia from my childhood, never allowed me to be hungry. My eating disorder, and upbringing, had me believing that only fat people got hungry. For most of my life, I believed that acknowledging my needs was unacceptable and invalid. My needs meant that I took up space. My identity was largely made up by how I saw my weight and my body, and my hunger was directly related to that. Ever since the morning of the jacket, I believed I was much bigger than everyone else. To me, the hungry-girl was always the fat girl. All of the skinny girls never seemed to be hungry, they never seemed to need anything. I never wanted to even eat in public because I didn't want people to see who I really was; a fat, smelly, unkempt, disrespected, stupid, gluttonous pig. All of this because I was hungry and taking care of myself by eating. I truly believed that the more I repressed my hunger, the skinnier I would appear. The skinner I would be.

In recovery, I had to allow myself to start feeling hunger. I had to start acknowledging that I am human. But I didn't know what it felt like. It started with what I thought was a stomach ache. I began feeling a cramping, a tingling, in my stomach that I had spent years repressing. I had come to feel that ache as a welcome emptiness, a good thing. When I sat with this ache, and described it out loud, it hurt. It was met with celebratory smiles and cheers.

"THAT'S HUNGER!" One of the other residents proclaimed, "Isn't that a crazy feeling? It hurts, but it doesn't hurt. It's been there all along, you've just been ignoring it!"

I was then challenged with balancing the experience of hunger and taking care of it appropriately- without overdoing it. I took four very specific, very elementary, steps at every meal so as to find this balance:

1. Discover and acknowledge hunger
2. Eat a healthy amount
3. Continue eating until satiated, but not overly full
4. Keep the meal in my stomach, which meant fighting the urges to purge

What I found was that I ran the risk of eating past the point of comfortable fullness and triggering my urges to purge. I also ran the risk of eating too little and triggering my urges to restrict. If I ate too little my eating disorder would gain power by feeling like I got away with restricting. Finding this balance, this place of comfort and power, took a lot of practice. It took all of my focus at every meal to stay mindful. I paid close attention to my satiety. My satiety level is when I feel like I've satisfied my needs, my body is happy and comfortable, but not uncomfortably full.

I had to stay mindful before and after every meal as well as every moment at the table. I used the hunger scale to determine how much to eat and to keep myself balanced. I've learned to keep myself between a 4-8 on the hunger scale at all times. If I go above an 8, it triggers a very strong urge to purge. If I go below a 4, it triggers my urges to keep restricting until I'm a 1. It's incredibly important for me to stay between a 4-8 on the hunger scale. This means constant snacks, not eating past the point of comfortable fullness, and not allowing myself to get hungry enough to trigger the urge to restrict.

At first this required unwavering focus and mindfulness while eating. One bite at a time. Really listening and feeling, detaching my body image issues and emotions from the food in front of me. Every moment took focus, even when I wasn't eating. I had to recognise hunger and deal with it appropriately, in a timely fashion, even when I wanted to distract myself with something else, or ignore it. Eventually it became a habit.

After years in recovery, this balance comes naturally.

I DARE TO LOOK INSIDE TO SEE WHAT IS KEEPING ME STUCK

Appeal of the eating disorder

As I separated myself out from the eating disorder, I was able to discover why it was so appealing to me and why it was so hard for me to let it go. It was appealing for countless reasons. My eating disorder made me feel powerful and competent. My eating disorder was something that was mine and no one else's. My eating disorder was a distraction from having to feel. My eating disorder was my escape. In every sense, my eating disorder was an addiction.

I always felt like I was powerful and in control when I was the best at something. I felt I was the best at my eating disorder. I loved being the best. To begin taking this power away from the eating disorder, I turned to other elements of my life that made me feel competent and powerful. I had to find control in other areas of my life in order not to focus on the eating disorder as an element of control in my life. I also had to discover why I needed the control in the first place.

I felt powerful and competent when helping others, running errands, educating people, riding my bike, and being outdoors. "Power" meant being able to achieve or get something I want. It meant being able and capable. "Power" meant having the ability to prove myself in any situation. "Power" meant having the ability to control a situation. My eating disorder made me feel all of these things. My eating disorder made me feel super-human in this sense. I had to begin to redirect myself and find new elements of my life that made me feel powerful.

In addition to acknowledging what made me feel powerful, I had to acknowledge the opposite as well: when I feel vulnerable or I've lost my feeling of control. I feel most vulnerable when others know I've messed up, made a mistake, when I don't know everything, or when others can see that I am not perfect. I feel vulnerable when others see that I have flaws.

I learned to sit with the discomfort of admitting that I don't know everything. I learned to sit and experience emotions, instead of using the eating disorder to cover them up. I learned to feel vulnerable and imperfect. I acknowledged that I will not always be in control. I will not always be the best at everything. I will not always be the most powerful in every situation. This has made me extremely uncomfortable many times over the years in my recovery.

Letting go of this illusion of control seemed impossible at first, but it did get easier with practice. In the past, I would have used these times of vulnerability to run back to the eating disorder. I would be able to tune-out the world and let the behaviors comfort my imperfect soul. Now that self destructive behaviors were no longer an option, I began to learn how to deal with the discomfort of highly emotional situations.

Another appeal of my eating disorder was that it made me feel unique. I thought I had something that no one else had, something no one else knew about. It gave me concrete goals to strive for. I felt like it was mine and I didn't have to share it with anyone- namely my mom and my sister. It was something I knew better than anyone else. When I was lonely, the behaviors and thoughts kept me occupied. Within it's grips, I felt like the world around me was tame and in control- even when it was spinning out of control and my addiction to weight loss grew.

Once I outlined and articulated why I was so drawn to my eating disorder, why it was so appealing to me, I could begin to find other, healthier ways to fulfill these needs. I found other things that made me feel powerful and in control. I found elements of my life that were mine that I didn't have to share with anyone. I found other activities and values that made me feel unique.

A huge emotional hurdle that I continue to struggle with to this day is having things in my life that I feel are *mine*. I need activities, core values, physical objects, and philosophies that I feel are mine, that I do not have to share with anyone. I grew up in a family that practiced very few emotional boundaries and I feel threatened when I believe someone is infringing on my space, or taking 'things' that are mine. The eating disorder filled this void, it was mine and no one else's. No one was copying or getting credit for my ideas, no one was mimicking me, no one was taking it from me, and this was something I experienced very little of in my childhood.

I have spent the last 10 years developing the ability to set boundaries with my friends and family. This enables me to have things in my life that are mine that I feel cannot be taken from me. I've learned that my personality is unique to me and I am an individual with much more to offer than an eating disorder. I speak up when coworkers or friends or family are taking credit for my ideas. I speak up when I need space and am not willing to share. I speak up when I feel infringed upon, or someone is copying me and it is making me uncomfortable. I still get irritated when I feel like people are piggybacking on my ideas and my lifestyle, but I speak up for myself and distance myself where it is necessary. Setting boundaries was extremely difficult at first and took lots of practice, but now it is a way of life for me. I have much more self-respect when I speak up and establish emotional boundaries with the people I choose to spend my time around.

To keep identifying the appeal of the eating disorder, and separating myself out from it, I went through every aspect of my life and developed a dynamic identity that is not based on weight or eating disordered behaviors. I discovered other elements in my life that were mine and familiar to me. I emphasized things that made me feel unique and gave me a healthy focus. As I filled these voids, the eating disorder continued to lose power.

I needed an eating disorder for many reasons. I use the term "punching bag" to express how I felt about my body. My eating disorder was able to use my body as an outlet to express emotions I never knew how to express. I did not learn how to acknowledge and express my emotions healthily in my childhood. Whether I wasn't getting enough attention or didn't understand that what I was feeling was frustration or betrayal or anger. My body became the way to express this. My body was a distraction from the emotions. I could focus on my body when I was sad, *"get thinner you'll be happy when you get thin."* I could focus on my body when I was angry, *"get thin, you'll find peace when you are thin. You can get revenge by becoming thin."* I could focus on my body when I was happy or excited, *"get thin, you'll feel even better than you do right now when you get thin."*

My body became the focus of every emotional need I had. It was a never-ending obsession, a perfect distraction and numbing tool. I was always able to focus on my body, always able to visualize myself in the ideal body. Melt away fat. Pinch it away. Become a stick figure. Deny food, deny needs, deny humanity. Every bite I denied made me more numb.

Then, when I couldn't take the denial anymore, I would fit as much food in my body as I possibly could. I was insatiable, I was infinitely needy. I would go from denying every need I ever had, to trying to satiate everything all at once. I would try to fill every void I ever experienced. I would eat so much, my jaw would ache when I chewed, and I couldn't stop eating. I was desperately hungry. Then, I'd go running to the nearest toilet, sink, drain, bucket, bag and vomit until I could taste bile, until I was lightheaded, until I could run my hand over my stomach convinced I was completely empty again. Convinced that I didn't need food, that I deserved the discomfort. Poised over the toilet, heaving out my insides, all I could think about was how guilty I'd felt for eating. It didn't matter how much I'd eaten, I just felt guilty for giving in. It would all be coming out anyways. I'd think about how shameful I'd been. Any bite was shameful, even one bite was too many. But during these cycles, I knew I was going to be throwing up, so why not eat two bites, or two meals, or three in one sitting?

By purging I could get rid of any shame I had from eating. I would get the adrenaline rush, the head rush, the feeling of fullness that made me unbearably uncomfortable followed by the immediate gratification of emptiness. The guilt attached to eating was so severe it was punishable by making myself sick, often more than twenty times a day. I used these behaviors to numb out the world around me, and distract myself from feeling any emotion. I would obsess about the food inside me. I couldn't focus if there was food in my stomach, I could only think of how I would get rid of it. No morsel got to stay inside. I would distract myself with the desperation for emptiness. I needed my eating disorder to get me through stressful situations because it was the only coping mechanism I had developed.

I knew my eating disorder better than anyone, it was my best friend. It was my worst enemy. I would do anything to please it, in turn it would reward me for a second *"you've done so good,"* and then set more goals for me, *"you can do better."* I went to it when I was happy, sad, mad, or lonely. It was the only being I felt had been with me my whole life, never leaving my side, always supporting me in the pursuit of the ideal body. Everyone could've abandoned me and I wouldn't have cared because I had my eating disorder. I had the behaviors to keep me occupied. I had the thoughts controlling me and keeping my brain distracted. It's extraordinarily sad when I think back at it- my best friend for almost 20 years was an eating disorder. Never allowing me to have real friends, never letting me have real experiences. Of course, that was part of the appeal at the time: never having to commit to anything real. Now, I'm furious when I think about how brain-washed I was. I missed out on having a healthy childhood and adolescence. I missed out on college experiences. I missed out on so much of my life as I was living it, all because I thought I had everything I needed in my eating disorder.

Developing healthy coping mechanisms has taken years of dedication to self improvement. The most effective strategies I developed came many, many years after my initial treatment time at CHS and I will elaborate on them in my discussion of Advanced Recovery.

While I was at CHS, I developed elementary coping skills. I learned about Dialectical Behavioral Therapy, Cognitive Behavioral Therapy, self care, and the effectiveness of labeling emotions and dealing with them in the moment. I learned about terms like, "kitchen sinking", which essentially means letting emotions pile up like dirty dishes in a sink. We learned how to deal with emotions as they surfaced, instead of trying to do the dishes all at once years from now. This has become a very effective relationship tool for me as well.

Dialectical Behavioral Therapy taught me how to regulate emotions in the moment and interact healthily with those around me. Some of the simple things I learned were how to recognise repetitive thought patterns and visualize these thoughts floating away instead of continuing to race and replay in my head. Another simple way I learned how to calm my anxiety was to focus on other sensations- smell, color, taste, feel, or sound. I discovered the calming nature of birds chirping and learned that I love peeling oranges when I am stressed- the color, the smell, the physical act, all of these sensations I learned would calm my nerves. I learned breathing techniques to get me through crisis-mode.

I learned that it is ok to speak up for myself when I am feeling a heightened emotion. I learned to identify and articulate these emotions and how to express them to those around me. Even if I didn't want to discuss the emotion, I learned how to say, "I am hurt. I am angry. Can we please talk about it?" Or "I am triggered, may I please have a second to work through it?" Eventually, I learned how to articulate my needs specifically to the people around me (coworkers, friends, relationships). I learned to teach people how to interact with me, instead of assuming they know what I need.

I learned to "catch it at simmer, not boil." A term used to describe dealing with emotions and interpersonal relationships. This means that as soon as I feel the twinge of an emotional reaction, I acknowledge it. I "catch it at simmer". I do not allow the uncomfortable emotion or interaction to continue until it overflows and is no longer manageable. This applies to many interactions and experiences in my life. In relationships, I speak up when something makes me upset or uncomfortable- instead of ignoring the issue until it boils over.

Most of my emotional regulation and disentangling at CHS was dialectical and cognitive behavioral therapies. I worked to become curious about my thoughts and thought patterns. I became curious about them. I questioned why I wanted to run to the bathroom to throw up, and it usually led me to see that I was experiencing a strong emotion that was making me uncomfortable.

In the initial stages of developing coping skills I learned the importance of identifying emotions. Once I put a label on a feeling, I could begin to heal it and process through it. I learned about "umbrella emotions", and realized that not everything I was feeling was anger. It was easy for me to label everything as anger or sadness. But I needed to dig deeper and be much more specific with my emotional identification. I learned that I feel frustration, betrayal, disappointment. Once I had a name for these emotions, it validated them and I could begin to process without the eating disorder behaviors.

I ACCEPT AND EXPERIENCE ALL OF MY FEELINGS

Reconnecting with Emotions

Part of being in treatment was reconnecting with my emotions. Emotions that I consistently had to deal with were anger, loneliness, boredom, depression, and anxiety. These were the emotions that surfaced most frequently for me. I had to sit with the discomfort of these emotions. I had to learn to talk through them instead of letting my urges disconnect me from reality. I learned to sit in the discomfort brought on by these emotions. I learned to talk about them. I learned to feel and understand the discomfort. I found new ways of dealing with my emotions instead of surrendering to the eating disordered urges that would surface.

At first, the urges were constant. An 'urge' is a strong desire to engage in eating disordered behaviors. For the first few weeks of treatment, I had urges every second of every day. Once I ceased indulging in the behaviors the urges lessened, but only slightly. From this point, I started discovering that almost every time I had an eating disordered thought or urge, it was connected to a strong emotion that I was trying to avoid or numb.

If I felt bored or lonely, I'd experience a strong urge to binge and purge. I wanted to cover up these uncomfortable emotions with eating disordered behaviors. If I was angry, I'd be overcome with the urge to restrict. If I was angry, I felt like I could hide, or get revenge on someone, by restricting. After recognizing the connection between emotions and fullness, I began looking internally at my emotional life when urges surfaced. I became curious about what was going on with my emotional state. My emotions made me feel full, which led me to want to restrict. I began to distinguish between emotional fullness and actual physical fullness. I'd frequently feel full of sadness, or anger, and truly believe I wasn't hungry.

Once, after a family session, a therapy session with my whole family, I felt full. I felt so full I felt like I would never be able to eat again. Family sessions were always difficult, upsetting, and triggering, but necessary. They made me full of emotion. For example, after a session with my dad once, after hearing him say a litany of things like, "your sickness," and "it's time for you to buck up," it made me feel like all of the information I'd given him was in vain. I felt like he wasn't taking me seriously. This desperately made me want to purge. I left that family session in a rage, desperate to throw up. I needed the release of the anger inside of me. I wanted to punish myself for being a nuisance to the family. Because I couldn't throw up, I went outside and threw rocks at trees and screamed. I was learning to deal with emotions that made me so uncomfortable that I wanted to tear my hair out.

Along with throwing rocks at trees, I discovered the power of throwing ice and punching pillows. All of these are harmless, and great ways to release pent up emotions. I discovered the power of screaming to release these pent up emotions as well. Once the initial waves of intense rage passed, I'd be able to talk about or journal about my emotions in a healthy fashion. Everytime I acknowledged my emotions instead of hiding them with an eating disorder, the eating disorder lost power.

I also had to get in touch with stillness and find peace in doing what I believed was "nothing". Being a perfectionist my whole life and always believing that I was unworthy, I was constantly going from activity to activity trying to prove my worth. I was always trying to prove to my parents, my family, my friends, my teachers, that I was worthy. I'd never sat still and listened to my thoughts. I never sat still and thought about my life, my journey, or my experiences.

I did a lot of processing on the days where I sat in a comfy chair in treatment doing "nothing". Many strong emotions surfaced when I was just sitting still. I had to learn to acknowledge and deal with boredom and loneliness.

My negative association with boredom stemmed from feeling unworthy. If I felt bored, I felt that I wasn't doing anything worthy. I felt I should be doing something to prove myself, prove my worth, perfect myself, or even improve the world. If I was bored, I wasn't doing anything except taking up space and wasting mine, and everyone else's time. I came to find that many moments of brilliance would come in the times when I was just sitting, contemplating my life.

It was as though a new consciousness began to develop in my head when I was doing "nothing". I learned to accept myself at any given moment, regardless of what I am "doing". I learned to accept myself from within, and not need the external validation that came along with constantly trying to prove my worth. I found that my boredom led me to be constantly trying to please others. I found that as long as I could stay in the present moment, accepting who I am, I learned to be at peace.

I had to be okay with being alone. My loneliness made me feel unworthy as well, because I believed that no one wanted to be with me. Part of learning to rid myself of this debilitating loneliness was acceptance; radical self-acceptance and acceptance of the notion that there is nothing wrong with me for being alone. There is nothing wrong with me if I am sitting alone. There is nothing wrong with me if I am eating alone. There is nothing wrong with me if I am engaging in activities alone. It was all part of the journey to accept myself and my personality just the way I am. When I radically accept myself from the inside, I can be alone and not need external acceptance or validation.

My journey of internal validation has consisted of lots and lots of practice. This has helped me mitigate my loneliness because I began enjoying my own company. When I wasn't constantly looking to others to prove my worth, when I wasn't constantly seeking the company of others for external validation, my loneliness lost its depressing power. Letting go of my desire for external validation helped me let go of my loneliness. This is an active process to this day. Even after years in recovery, I need to remain vigilant so I do not find myself constantly seeking external approval.

At first, I didn't realize I was experiencing anxiety. I didn't know what the feeling was, my brain would shut down and I couldn't think, I couldn't listen, and I lost my ability to make decisions. My vision would get blurry and I would feel dizzy and dehydrated. I did not know this was anxiety. I thought something was wrong with me. I felt like someone was scratching at the inside of my ribcage. I had experienced this feeling as a child and an adolescent. I had always thought there was something wrong with me and I was always worried that this surreal feeling would overcome, and paralyze, me. Now, I felt it when we would go out to lunch in restaurants and I felt it during family sessions. I began to see the correlation between engaging in big challenges with food and therapy, and this odd sensation that overcame me.

"That's anxiety!" Someone proclaimed when I described the sensations in my body, thinking there was something physically wrong with me.

Up until then, I thought anxiety was something only experienced by people with stressful jobs, or single mothers, or people who were 'weak-minded'. But I heard someone describing what they were calling 'anxiety' and it sounded exactly like what I was experiencing. And suddenly I had the vocabulary to deal with what I was experiencing. It was a huge relief to find out that there was nothing wrong with me, it was anxiety.

Once I had a label for this feeling, I was able to start dealing with it. I could say, "I'm feeling anxious…" and the people around me would understand. They were able to talk to me about it and help me through it. They would ask me questions about what exactly was causing the anxiety. Sometimes, all I needed to do was verbalize the fact that I was anxious to get me through a situation. This was the case in any situation involving emotions. Verbalizing my emotions, fears, or urges always helped. Hearing myself say my thoughts out loud always helped. Verbalizing what was going on in my head, with the eating disorder, always took power away from the eating disorder.

My eating disorder thrived on secrecy, so everytime I verbalized my eating disordered thoughts, the eating disorder would lose power.

Once I had the vocabulary to express my anxiety, my frustrations, and my disappointments, I could talk about these emotions and process them properly. I was learning how to calm myself down without the eating disorder.

I WILL LET MYSELF RECEIVE THE HEALING I NEED

Depression & Bipolar Disorder

While in treatment I was diagnosed with mild Bipolar Depression. I was put on mood stabilizers and antidepressants. There is a common thread between eating disorders and mood disorders. In the past I, unknowingly, tried to regulate and stabilize my moods with eating disordered behaviors.

I felt my depression, at the time, as a heavy, overwhelming sense of hopelessness. I couldn't imagine getting through the days. When I am depressed, I don't want to participate in my life. Nothing brings me joy and I'm exhausted. The lack of energy that comes along with my depression makes me want to sleep all day, everyday. And then I feel guilty for wanting to sleep, the guilt makes me more depressed, and on and on.

Being bipolar means I cycle through episodes of this depression and mania. My manic episodes (I refer to these swings as being "high" or "low") include an increase in energy and desire to be social. When I'm "high" I feel compelled to keep myself busy and am fueled by a frenetic, anxious, energy. When I am "low" I feel as though I can't accomplish anything and every little task takes all of my energy. I used my addiction, my eating disordered behaviors to attempt to regulate these mood swings and escape from the highs and lows. I didn't know it at the time, but these swings were contributing to my extreme emotional discomfort. If I was depressed, I could escape the depression by bingeing and purging, or I could comfort my hopelessness by restricting. The depression added to my feelings of worthlessness and lack of control in my life. I felt like I could regain my control by restricting, controlling my food intake. If I was high, I could use the extra energy to binge and purge or over-exercise. By the end of a binge/purge cycle I would feel tranquilized, my adrenaline would be released, and I would be lulled into feeling slightly normal again.

I regulated my moods with medication for many years. The cocktail of meds I was on was constantly changing to find the right balance for my brain chemistry. Though I feel like I never found the proper balance, I felt that these meds were helpful and I am very glad I was taking them.

I stopped taking the medications about 5 years after my discharge. I was experiencing a very deep depressive episode and became so frustrated with psychiatrists and therapists, that I stopped taking my meds. I chose to turn to meditation and journaling instead. I was determined to find my inner peace without medications. In hindsight, this was a dangerous decision for me to make without the help of a medical professional. I went through a very rough transition, as I did not wean myself off of the meds as I should have. I stopped taking them and had extreme withdrawal symptoms. My anxiety was almost unbearable, and I experienced physical symptoms as well. For example, my eyes stopped tracking with my head movements, so my vision was compromised and I felt car sick for a couple weeks. I stayed in bed, or close to my home, for three weeks as these symptoms abided.

Regardless, I began to dissect my life and attempt to design it so I could regulate my moods and eliminate triggers for depression. One of my triggers is exhaustion and stress at work. At the time, I was in a management position in a company I had been working for for several years. I quit this job as it was bringing me far too much stress and the stress was triggering my depression. I found an entry level job in my field, one that was enjoyable, not stressful, and was able to quiet my mind enough to begin to explore what I needed to do to stabilize my moods without meds.

This has been a very long process over the years. I have found that I still cycle. A stressful event will trigger a mood swing, usually depression. This "low" lasts about 6-8 weeks and then I cycle into a few weeks of heightened energy levels. I know and understand these cycles. I feel and am familiar with these cycles to my core.

The most helpful thing I have discovered is to pay attention and not fight my moods. If I am depressed, I acknowledge it. I take extra good care of myself, get plenty of rest, and radically accept that it will not always feel the way that it does. When I am experiencing a "high", I embrace the extra energy. I allow myself to be more social, to accomplish tasks, and benefit from the swing. This has taken many years of practice, and is probably not what doctors recommend, but I have made it work for me. I am very in tune with my emotional state, my internal life, and my self-care practices. I listen to my body and take care of myself without self harm and without being dangerous to myself or those around me.

Meditation and journaling have been the most helpful for this. I discover depths of my emotional state, my soul, and my personality that I never knew existed when I journal. The stillness in meditation helps me quiet my mind and listen to my higher self for guidance. I will elaborate on the importance of journaling in Advanced Recovery.

I WILL TAKE TIME TO HONOR
AND EXPRESS MY DREAMS

Treatment takes time

I am blessed beyond measure that I was able to stay in treatment for as long as I did. I was at CHS for over three months. One hundred and one days to be exact. While I was there women came and went. Some left and came back. I met women with varying degrees of eating disorders, but a constant theme I witnessed was that women left the Center too early in their treatment process. They left for various reasons; some wanted to go back to school, some needed to get back to their families, but the majority of them left because insurance was no longer covering their residential treatment. They had to leave because their insurance kicked them out. Insurance refused to pay for their stay.

It is typical for insurance companies to stop paying for treatment when an individual is considered "stable". When an individual begins to eat again and their vitals normalize. When someone stops purging. Insurance companies act as though once the eating disordered behaviors cease in a regulated environment, the eating disorder is treated. But this is merely the first step in a very long process. I remember joking with a fellow resident once, "Of course we're eating! If we don't eat, they send us to West Hills!" West Hills was the mental institution up the street that we were all terrified of being sent to. Of course I stopped purging, my bathroom visits were monitored.

Watching this cycle of women coming and going and returning constantly reminded me that eating disorders are not about the behaviors. The behaviors are a manifestation of emotional dysfunction. It takes time to disentangle why the behaviors are there in the first place and why the eating disorder is necessary, why the addiction is there to begin with.

Relapse is high with eating disorders because these individuals didn't get enough time in treatment to discover how their eating disorder is

serving them, why they need it, and how to replace self-destructive behaviors with nurturing ones.

Along with the time, there are many social implications and questions about how and when to "come out" with your eating disorder.
There was the constant worry about what to tell people about our struggles and when. Constant questions included, "Who do I tell?" "What do
I say when people ask where I've been?" "What if someone notices my
weight gain?"

These questions are secondary to any type of functional recovery,
but they are very important to address, as many of our appearances
changed while we were at treatment. Many people had to go back to jobs,
to school, back to family. The most helpful piece of advice I was given
was that I do not owe anyone anything. I do not owe anyone an explanation. I was reassured that I would know who to tell, how much to
reveal, and when. I was encouraged to trust myself to know if and when
I needed or desired to reveal my struggles. At the time, I didn't trust my
judgements, I did not trust myself, my emotional stability, or my boundary setting abilities, so this piece of advice seemed useless.

When I left treatment, and over the last few years, it has proven true.
I know what to say, who to say it to, and practiced revealing my struggles
in a way that invited discussion around eating disorders and recovery.
When I first left treatment, I almost felt as though I owed everyone I
came in contact with an explanation for where I had been. I was still
separating myself out from the eating disorder, developing my new identity, but it was still a huge piece of who I was. I have learned that I do
not owe anyone anything. No one needs to know about my struggles
unless I feel compelled to reveal them. I learned the verbiage that I use
with confidence now.

Many of the girls in treatment felt like they had to tell everyone and
were terrified as their eating disorder was their deep, shameful secret. My
therapist told me, "I bet you'll be surprised as to how many people already know. Even without you telling them. People figure these things
out and they are probably so proud of you for what you are doing to help
yourself. These people probably saw you struggling, didn't know what
to say, were extremely worried about you, and are so proud of you. They
will never understand your struggles, it is not your responsibility to try
and make them understand."

I grew into knowing exactly who to tell and what to say. I don't have shame around my eating disorder, but I didn't tell people until they had earned the knowledge. Until I knew I could trust them when I was feeling vulnerable. Especially in the early days of recovery, I felt that the more people who knew my battles, it was more room for people to involve themselves and I needed space to own my recovery.

Over the years, it has become less of a reveal of a huge secret to a casual mention of my past struggles, my pride in my recovery, and an invitation for discussion. It is important for the people in our lives to know when we are struggling and how they can help, also being able to open the lines of communication regarding triggers is a very important piece of involving others in my recovery.

Some helpful phrases I've found over the years are:

- I struggled with an eating disorder for a very long time, I'm doing great with it now, and I'm really proud of myself
- That comment was very triggering. When you say... Here is what I heard... would you mind clarifying your statement for me?
- I'm triggered right now, can I talk to you about it?
- I'm totally open to talking about it because I'm in a really good place
- I'm kind of struggling right now, I need space to figure it out, can I talk to you about it later?
- Recovery was the hardest thing I've ever imagined myself going through, here's what helped...

Ultimately everyone decides how much they are willing to reveal to others about their struggles. It can be helpful, but it does have the potential to be harmful. Trust yourself, that you will know, and do not feel obligated to share anything with anyone until you are comfortable.

I WILL SURROUND MYSELF WITH PEOPLE
WHO ARE AFFIRMING AND ENCOURAGING

Family therapy, roles, and dynamics

Family therapy was an extremely difficult, but very necessary, piece of my treatment and recovery. I had to delve deep into my past and discover that eating disorders are a family illness. This means that family dynamics and the family system have a role in the development of an eating disorder. It also means that the entire family system is affected by an eating disorder.

I did a creative representation of my family, and through this medium, through this collage, I discovered that I've always felt like the outcast of my family. The representation included a clown on a tightrope (me), entertaining everyone, making sure everyone was laughing. My mom was at the base of the collage balancing everyone, holding everything up. There was a bookworm on top of a stack of books (my sister). My mom's partner Susan was represented with me, playing off on the side, as representations of my mom and my sister jeered at us from across the page. Perfectly balanced. Everyone in their places, everyone playing their roles. My family laughed when I showed this representation to them, it was painfully accurate.

Then, my family members were asked to sketch how they envisioned the family as well. My mother's sketch was astounding. She drew me as a dust devil, a tornado, unpredictable, and wild. She drew my sister as a perfectly square box. Always small and predictable. These drawings help us define why we had such a hard time dealing with each other growing up. I understood that my family saw me as wild and unpredictable; I was hard to manage, a tornado, an unstoppable force to be reckoned with.

My sister was upset about the sketch and went and got her ear pierced the next week- that was "out of the box" for her at the time. Family therapy uncovered issues for everyone. We related to these sketches, and were affected so deeply by their accuracy, because these were the versions of ourselves we were allowed to be within the family unit. These were the roles we played and fit into, with the knowledge that we would not be accepted if we strayed from these versions of ourselves.

Growing up, my sister was easy to manage and I was considerably more difficult. It was easier for my family (my parents) to punish and fight with me, than to reason with me. This history, and habit, of conflict led me to feel like an outcast. This led me to feel as though I wasn't getting enough attention, or that my emotional needs weren't being met. My eating disorder developed partially out of these patterns and family dynamics. The dynamics had me feeling like an outcast and needing a way to deal with the emotions that came along with feeling left out.

I was an emotional child, and my emotions confused me because we never talked about them in the moment. If I was mad or frustrated or sad, we would put it on a list of things to be discussed at our next family meeting. Therefore, I did not learn how to deal with intense emotions the minute they surfaced, I learned to talk about them a few days later, if at all. I had a lot of anger and sadness surrounding my parents divorce, but these emotions confused me because I was not allowed to express them in the moment.

I relied on the eating disorder as a coping mechanism to deal with these emotions. It became my friend when no one else understood. It gave me a distraction and something to hide behind when the emotions became too much for me. I did not learn how to deal with intense emotions as a child. When my mother thought I was 'too much' and didn't want to deal with me, I could focus on my weight instead. I focused on food to distract me from the emotions that came along with the pain of my parents divorce, the need to appear perfect through the trauma, and the inability to process emotions.

I came to the realization that I felt like I'd made my mom suffer my whole life. She always seemed to have an easy time with my sister, and I've always felt like a nuisance. The eating disorder helped me cope with this in countless ways. I helped bring control back when I felt everything was out of my control. When my mom was upset with me, I could disappear into it.

I started mismanaging my emotions at a very young age, which contributed to the development of the eating disorder. My mother claims that I used to turn into what she called "The Beast,". The Beast was an out of control, temper tantrum throwing, "pill" of a child. I remember throwing these fits and having many screaming fights with my mother. Through much therapy, we've discovered that The Beast was a coping mechanism. It was a way of channeling my emotional needs as they were being ignored. Whether I saw my actions as malevolent, or not, The Beast was a defense mechanism used to process the intense emotions I was feeling as a child. My anger and desire to be listened to slowly morphed into an eating disorder.

In order to heal, I started identifying patterns in my family. My mother always came at me expecting a fight and my other family members usually expected conflict when approaching me. I painfully learned that nothing was ever easy for my family members when it came to interacting with me.

Providing humor at the expense of my emotional well-being was another mechanism I used to process, and ultimately deny, emotions. I was always able to provide my family a distraction from a serious situation with a joke or a story of my self-sabotage. Because of this, my family rarely took me seriously. My life was a source of humor, and entertainment, for my family. I provided a method for the family system to communicate: humor. I'm the joke. I've always been able to lighten situations and offer the family something to make fun of, something to find flaws in. I was something to watch and scrutinize and be a living excuse for failure. I provided balance in the family system by indulging my family members in this lack of reality. We could joke about how I was meeting the expectation of failure.

I learned a lot in family therapy, about the roles we play, how my personality developed, and how it contributed to the development of the eating disorder. Regarding the roles in my family, my mother has always been the strongest . In the past, when she displayed any emotion, I used to feel as though it was my fault. As though I had caused her grief in some way. When my mom let her guard down enough to feel emotions, or her weakness showed I would feel guilty. I used to think vulnerability and emotions were weaknesses. Growing up, when my mom felt negative emotions, I felt as though I had let her down. I felt that if my mom was affected, we were no longer safe as a family. When my mom was angry, I felt that I needed to hide and get out of her way. It used to be difficult to see my mother affected by things because I thought this was a sign of weakness, or loss of control. When my mom experienced emotions, I felt like suddenly everything was out of control. I rarely witnessed my mom actually experiencing emotions. She would put up a wall, her edge, to keep herself safe. When I got around that wall, I had done something catastrophic, enough to glean emotion from my mom. I hated feeling like I was always letting her down in some way.

A few other sessions that were poignant were those with my dad and his wife and our collective dynamic. I feel like I never really got my dad to understand eating disorders, but I also don't believe he tried. I don't blame him, my experience has been that it is very difficult to understand eating disorders. Most people will never understand them at all. For the most part, external witnesses don't understand why I don't just eat. My dad didn't ask questions, because it made him look weak or inferior. I always used to go to my dad for questions I needed a confident answer on. He always seemed to know everything. But he didn't take the time to inquire about eating disorders, even though it would have been helpful. He wanted the issue to be "solved." He wanted me to be "fixed". He didn't have the answers, and my dad hated not having the answer. He liked to feel like he knew everything, he was always the hero in all of his stories. When he was confronted with something he didn't know anything about, he shut down and acted terribly insensitive.

Eating disorders are illogical, and it was difficult for the people who love me to watch me experience something they couldn't label or fix. I didn't expect my dad to understand, but I would have liked him to ask questions. I would have liked him to be vulnerable and admit that he didn't know everything. Instead, our sessions consisted of him using phrases referring to my "sickness". He used phrases like "fix your problem" and "when you've gained weight back." These phrases were not helpful or supportive, I felt shamed and confused. I asked him to research eating disorders. I sent him books. I reiterated that it wasn't about gaining weight and that I didn't have a "problem." I tried explaining that my eating disorder was a manifestation of dysfunctional family dynamics. Though I tried, I never felt we were able to find a language that expressed love and understanding about my eating disorder. He did attend family sessions and I found them helpful for my own growth and understanding.

We agreed that we spoke completely different languages as people. We agreed that he did not have as much in common with me as he did with my sister. He admitted to favoring my sister through my childhood. It validated how I had been feeling and answered questions I had from my childhood. I was able to start labeling and untangling why I always felt left out when we visited our dad's house.

My dad inadvertently helped me come up with an image I use to describe eating disorders to this day. We were discussing his wife and my interactions with her. I have never gotten along with my dad's wife. I have always felt that she fostered an environment for competition for my dad's love. I felt she was disrespectful to our family and, as a child, I felt like she was stealing my dad. The complexities of the eating disorder and family dynamics had still not found their way into my dad's understanding. It was clear to me when he said, "When you're around her, can't you just put on a Haz Mat suit for protection or something?" This was his sarcastic way of asking me to become someone I'm not in order to tolerate his wife's behavior, not internalize it, and not take her behavior personally. It was him asking me to ignore how much I dislike her and fake that we all got along.

It was as though a huge light bulb exploded in my head. An eating disorder is a very dysfunctional form of an emotional Haz Mat suit. It is a neutralizing, protective, suit to deal with the emotional hazards I encountered in my life. My eating disorder was my coping mechanism to deal with the toxicity in my life.

Thanks, Dad! Yes, I have been putting on my Haz Mat suit for years. This is what my protective shield looks like. No emotions get in, no emotions get out. I live and breathe the air of a woman who only has to think about starving and bingeing and purging. I am protected from emotions. Actually, Dad, using the analogy of a Haz Mat for an eating disorder is perfect. Every time I was around my dad and his wife, I was able to put my eating disorder on. I had my biohazard suit to protect me from toxic environments. I used my eating disorder to protect me from feeling the deep emotional pain I felt in my dad's company. I used it in every aspect of my life as well.

As a way of organizing thoughts and emotions, I began writing letters to people with zero intent of actually sending them. A lot of these letters were written to my dad. The letters highlighted him choosing his wife over my sister and I. They addressed the lack of attention in my childhood. The letters explained that I was not at summer camp to gain weight, that I don't need to "buck up," and be tough all the time. They explained my need to begin acknowledging and feeling emotions instead of ignoring my pain. These letters explained that trying to cover up my pain was making it worse.

I've spent over 10 years developing coping mechanisms because I did not learn how to deal with emotions as a child. As a child, I learned how to "buck up" and be tough. I learned that "it's just pain," and it will pass. I learned to not acknowledge my physical or emotional pain and taught myself how to channel it into dysfunctional behaviors instead.

Growing up there was a lot of family pressure to appear perfect, especially around my grandparents and their friends. When my mom and dad got divorced, my mom's parents stopped speaking to us as a family for a few years. When they began speaking to us again, I felt as though we had to win them back. There was an extraordinary need to be perfect. The family needed to seem as though we were doing perfectly. It had to appear that my mom was doing a perfect job raising her perfect children. The bar was extraordinarily high for my sister and I to appear flawless in every setting; at dinners, at school functions, in meetings. We were to be the most mature, the most polite, and the most functional family on all occasions. We were always on our best behavior, we got the best grades, we participated in school functions and extracurricular activities. We would ask for extra homework from our advanced course teachers if we still did not feel challenged.

This pressure to appear perfect created another dynamic of our family system. Under all of this pressure, the eating disorder continued to manifest itself throughout my childhood and adolescence. My eating disorder was a way to control my behavior, to appear perfect. There was always something to strive for, I'd never be good enough. I'd never accomplish the goals I'd set before me. I'd never be the perfect child my parents wanted me to be. I'd never be as mature or as smart as I should be. But the eating disorder gave me something to strive for that I felt like I could accomplish. These were goals that made sense to me and I thought my family would be proud of. I was possessive of my diets and weight goals. My diets were mine and I felt like I designed the way they worked. I was better at dieting than my sister, which was rewarding beyond measure.

I knew that once I was discharged from CHS, and returned back to the family system, I would be responsible for behaving differently and implementing all of the lessons I had learned. I had the knowledge and responsibility to change the family dynamics. I knew that falling back into old family patterns could lead me back into relying on old behaviors. Shifting the family dynamic was up to me. I knew I'd have to go back to my family and behave differently. Behave differently, set boundaries, and teach them how I wanted to be treated; as a grown up, mature woman. Not a joke. Not a scapegoat. Not a younger sibling. A woman who has taken responsibility to change.

It took a lot of courage to return to my family and begin asserting myself, speaking my emotions aloud when necessary. My family began to respect me as a mature adult. I asked them to trust and respect me. They began giving me space to make decisions and follow through with my own ideas.

I even began pointing out when my family was falling back into dysfunctional patterns. To this day, this still requires an extraordinary amount of courage and practice. I started by pointing out when we were trying to be perfect. I began taking the initiative to have hard conversations and deal with tough emotions. I took the initiative to stop minimizing myself to fit into their idea of what I should be. I stopped making jokes about my short-comings to appease my family. I created a new concept of myself and projected it outward, hoping my family would follow my lead. I began helping my family gain perspective and learn how to set boundaries. With a clear sense of boundaries, what is mine, what is yours, we each began experiencing the world on our own. We each became entitled to our own individual emotions. We were able to explore our own personalities without needing validation from the rest of the family.

Over the past 10 years, I have become a Queen of Boundaries. I know where I begin and where others start. I know what I deserve and I know how to verbalize it. I have a clear sense of self and practice verbalizing my needs. Having good boundaries means knowing exactly how I need to be interacted with and having the verbiage to ask for it from those around me. Having boundaries means knowing that I have things; ideas, places, emotions, that are mine and I am entitled to have them. I am allowed to have these things that are mine. Boundaries take practice.

When I entered treatment, I had no boundaries. I believed that everyone else's thoughts and emotions were what I was supposed to be feeling. I had no idea who I was, what emotions were actually mine, or even how to recognise and take care of my own needs. I didn't know how to assert myself to protect my well being.

My first lesson in boundaries came from the horses at Espiritu Ranch in Gardnerville, NV. We were blessed enough to attend equine therapy (horse therapy) every weekend. Equine Assisted Therapy uses animals to teach individuals recovering from addictions to develop new social skills including creative problem solving, facing fears, setting boundaries, and building confidence and self esteem. I looked forward to the time I got to spend with the horses every week. I discovered aspects of my personality that I don't believe I could have without the horses.

The most memorable, most influential exercise for me was one regarding boundaries. In this exercise, we were given a stack of sticky notes. On them we wrote down things we wanted to protect; including aspects of our personalities, our favorite activities, our love for our families, and our values. On my sticky notes were things like, "my creativity," "my athleticism," "my sense of humor," "my relationships," "my ability to love," "my eating disorder." We stuck our sticky notes to orange traffic cones and were instructed to protect the cones from the horses. We were supposed to keep the horses from touching the cones. What we didn't know is that the horse's favorite toy was the traffic cone. At first it was really hard to keep the horse away from his favorite toy. I felt like an awful person trying to protect what was mine (my sticky notes on the traffic cone). We tried distracting him by petting him and giving him other toys. Nothing worked to keep this gigantic animal away from the traffic cone.

"Protect what's yours, don't let him take what's yours," the therapist kept saying. All of us struggling to distract or come up with another idea of how to keep the horse away.

I finally ended up physically pushing the horse away from the cone. Boundary established.

He wandered off to the other side of the arena. I instantly felt like a terrible person, I felt like I had hurt the horse's feelings and that he was going to be mad at me. I had protected what was mine, I had accomplished the goal, but I wanted the horse to like me. I felt horribly guilty for being so strong in my intentions and protecting my values. About 30 seconds later, the horse came back and started chewing on my shoelaces. I pet him and started laughing. "You can have my shoelaces."

I felt as though he was making peace with me. I felt like he was my buddy and he wasn't going to invade my sacred space anymore. He was proud of me for protecting what I needed to protect and was coming back to show that he respected me more because of it.

I have remembered this lesson in every single relationship, job, and friendship I have had since that day.

I began looking at how I could apply this lesson and reflect it into human relationships. This experience showed me that I can know what I need to protect, set boundaries, and stand up for them without feeling guilty. I learned that I do not need to feel guilty for taking care of my needs. In fact, the horse showed me that he had more respect for me because I set a boundary. He indicated that we could be closer friends because of it. I took this lesson back to my family and began to practice setting good boundaries and protecting my emotions.

I helped my family learn that emotions cannot be scheduled or structured, like we used to do in the past. Emotions are immediate and messy. My family began to learn that we cannot be constantly hiding behind our desire for perfection. We learned valuable communication skills so we could begin verbalizing our needs through high stakes emotions.

Communication began replacing the eating disorder as a valuable coping mechanism. I learned to talk about my anger, not hide it. I learned to verbalize my shame, and not numb it. I learned to communicate my desire for perfection and talk about my short-comings. Every time I communicated or verbalized an emotion, it validated it, made it real, and took power away from the eating disorder. I also learned to discern what emotions were necessary to share with my family, and which ones needed to be processed with a therapist. This distinction was very important, because it allowed me to have my own emotional life, my own emotional experiences without needing it to be validated by my family.

Another coping mechanism I relied on to process my emotions was comedy. I helped my family to understand and support me in channeling this in a healthy way. Previously, I provoked shaming laughter at my shortcomings, and at my failures, I desired to turn my experiences into a comedy routine for everyone else's entertainment. I had to learn to be comfortable experiencing any emotion that surfaced without degrading myself for others' entertainment. I began to deal with the emotions instead of turning them into a spectacle or a laughing stock.

In my advanced stages of recovery, many years after treatment, I learned that I am truly funny. That I genuinely love making people laugh. But it is because I am smart and witty, not because I have no other way to process the emotion.

I began redefining my relationships with each member of the family. Redefining my relationship I had with my sister meant standing up for myself when my mom and my sister ganged up on me. It meant knowing that I didn't have to fulfill the role of "little sister" anymore. I no longer accepted being the scapegoat. I made a point to act mature, so I was not easily labeled as the joker of the family or the younger sibling. I gave my sister reasons to take me seriously as a young woman and did not stand for my family members making fun of me without my permission.

To redefine my relationship with my mother, I had to disconnect myself from her fear of being fat. I had to disconnect myself from her food fears that were projected onto us as kids. As kids, we learned that food was supposed to be bland. We learned to never indulge. We learned to eat less than you need. We learned that eating was a chore.

In treatment, I learned that it is not my job to fight my mother's fears about obesity, my job is to keep myself healthy. It meant completely disconnecting from fears of perfection and food, and re-entering the relationship with my own ideas about food. It meant maintaining a renewed relationship with my body size and my own views on the pursuit of perfection, regardless of my mother's perspective. It meant, once again, communicating my feelings and setting boundaries so I could take care of myself.

It was a lot of responsibility to return to these relationships with changed views. I had to continue to observe and assert myself, and stand up for my points of view. It was extremely challenging to break a lifelong pattern of habitual family dysfunction. But once one person begins to change, the whole system has to change. It took repetition, courage, and practice to continue to assert myself and form new habits within the family. All of these changes led to new forms of communication. Once these lines of communication were open, we began to talk freely about our food fears, body fears, and imperfections among the family.

Redefining my relationship with my dad required us to admit that he blatantly favored my sister when we were growing up. We both agreed that this favoritism would typically lead me to isolate when we were all together. I've always liken my father's presence in my life to that of a sport's fan. He was there for the big games, the performances, the graduations, all the happy events, but he missed all the hard work and life behind each event. He missed practices behind big games. He missed heart breaks, homework, and paper writing. He missed all the big decisions. Every so often we'd chat and he would get a 'play by play' of my life, but wasn't an active participant.

At the time of my treatment and recovery, I found his presence in my life to be toxic. I learned in treatment that there will be people in my life who are toxic and I learned to set boundaries to protect myself from that toxicity invading my life. My boundary with my dad was lowering my expectations of him and not expecting anything more than a call every few months to catch up. I didn't go to my dad with help making big decisions or seeking moral support.

A couple years into my recovery, I tried to make an effort with my dad, to put him into my immediate communication circle. I tried to put him in the list of people I communicate with regularly when I just want to chat. I began calling my dad to try to involve him in more of my life. I did this for awhile, but eventually had to distance myself, once again, because he would inadvertently say insensitive things that were still difficult for my brain to process healthily. He would make comments that would indicate to me that he hadn't done any research on eating disorders, and therefore didn't care about the experience I was going through.

My relationship with my dad changed many years later, during the initial phases of the COVID pandemic and then through his battle with lung cancer which ultimately took his life. I stopped looking to my dad for moral or emotional support, I learned that there are very specific things I can talk to and bond with my dad about. Those things did not include my experiences with my eating disorder. However, in his last days, I held a barf bag for him as he was throwing up and made a bulimia joke. I said, "Don't worry, Dad, I am a Vomit Expert." My dad looked up at me and grinned. He grinned like he understood exactly what I was saying and finally understood my grim sense of humor. I was not making a joke of myself, I was proudly owning my experiences, my lessons, offering humor, and supporting my dad in his final days.

My ultimate lesson in redefining relationships, learning to communicate, and setting good boundaries boils down to my authenticity. It means being true to myself. It means I know what I want, and I know how to verbalize it. And I know I deserve it. It means trusting that I know what is healthy for me. It means I know my core values and my truths. It means standing up for myself. It means teaching people how to treat me and interact with me. It means asserting myself in public and creating a life without an eating disorder.

Through years of practice, I know myself very well. I know my expectations of myself and how to live up to them. Along with knowing what I want, I forgive myself and admit when I am not exactly sure. I am honest with myself. Everytime I act in line with my authentic-true self, I feel the eating disorder losing power. Everytime I listen to my own wholesome thoughts, the eating disorder loses power. My eating disorder wanted me to use it to cope with family dysfunction, but every time I refuse to hide my personality, my emotions, or my shame using the eating disorder, it loses power.

I didn't start my childhood with an eating disorder. I wasn't born with the need to restrict, binge, purge, and overexercise. I started out with family dysfunction, pressure to be perfect, and a deeply ingrained fear of being fat. I had a deep desire to have boundaries, something that was mine and not my sister's, but had no idea how to cope and develop. This created a maelstrom for the eating disorder.

I AM IN CHARGE OF MY LIFE

Discharge from CHS

As soon as I packed up, said a tearful goodbye, and drove away from the Center, I began laughing and crying uncontrollably. I was overwhelmed with emotion. I was overwhelmed with pride, excitement, and fear about my new life. Even though it was 6 o'clock at night, I went to Starbucks and got a huge cup of coffee to celebrate my freedom. I drank it as I drove home and settled into my new living space. I ate a dinner of frozen pizza, with veggies, and read until I fell asleep.

It felt so normal. I was very much at peace, though my head was racing with fears and anxieties about my new life, "Could I make it on my own?" "How long could I go without being triggered and having urges?" "Will I remember everything I've learned and worked so hard for?"

The next day I would go grocery shopping to supply myself with everything I needed for my new life.

I was challenged with keeping food in the house for nourishment. In the past I would have never been able to imagine having food in the cupboards and not bingeing. I made another deal with myself that I would go to the grocery store and purchase food for my *nourishment*. I would no longer purchase food with the intention of bingeing on it. I forced myself to be calm while there was food sitting in cupboards. I continued telling myself that the food could be there without me needing to binge as a distraction from boredom or loneliness. I challenged myself to take initiative and eat when I was hungry, and eat what my body was craving. I practiced eating alone without allowing the guilt to creep in. I began to allow myself to eat without feeling like I needed to compensate by overexercising and purging.

While in treatment, there was a schedule and other residents to encourage strict meal times. There was always company at snack time.

Someone was always there to talk with me while I ate, I never had to eat alone. After discharge, I was on my own; looking at the clock, listening to my body, setting alarms for meals when I needed to. There was no external stimulus to prompt meal times, and I had to trust that my body was enough. I had to accept that I would have to eat, and take care of my body, without permission or seeking justification. I had to completely surrender to my intuitive eating process.

Intuitive eating has taken years of practice. It is the process of eating when hungry and stopping when full. It sounds simple, but it is the process of unraveling years of societal & social programming. Intuitive eating is how we ate as kids, it is how kids eat before society invades our minds with an addiction to dieting.

Evelyn Tribole & Elyse Resch present this concept in their book, *Intuitive Eating*. They present the idea of eating the food that your body is craving and eating to a point of satiety. Satiety is being full to a point of satisfaction- not overly stuffed, just comfortably full. Chronic dieters are fully aware of the cycle of restricting until hunger takes over and then eating to a fullness level that causes discomfort. Deprivation often leads to a binge cycle. When I would go several weeks, or months, or even years severely depriving myself, it would always lead me to binge.

Tribole and Resch also present the idea of a Food Police. The Food Police is the voice in our heads that classifies us as good or bad based on food choices. Because my Food Police was so strong, it took years of getting in tune with my fullness and hunger levels as well as my emotional state. It took a heightened sense of mindfulness and granting myself unconditional permission to eat when I was hungry. I had to sit down to every meal, completely aware of my emotions, knowing that they could make me feel full or empty and lead me to want to distract and hide behind food. Intuitive Eating, like the entire recovery process, took courage, faith, and patience.

Part of my lesson with Intuitive Eating was realizing and accepting that there would always be food. Always. I would never have to starve again. I had to tell myself over and over that I am always allowed to eat when I am hungry. I frequently had the feeling that I'd never be permitted to eat again. I'd spent so much of my life dieting and depriving myself, that I always felt as though, when I was eating, it would be the last time my eating disorder was ever going to let me eat. As a result, I'd eat until I was uncomfortably full. Then, I would hate myself for bingeing.

Once I began to let go of the fear of starving- the fear of never being allowed to eat again- I gave myself permission to eat anytime I was hungry. I began recognising when I was full or content. I was able to recognize when I had had enough of what I was eating and I was satiated.

I began recognizing other feelings as well: when my body had gotten the proper nutrients, what I was craving, and how much. This is an ongoing practice in mindfulness. I never wanted to eat past the point of comfortably full because it triggered my desire to purge. But I also had to make sure I was eating enough, so as not to trigger my desire to restrict.

This was extremely challenging at first, because I always felt as though I was eating too much. My brain, and the remaining eating disorder thoughts, would tell me I was eating too much, yet my body was still hungry. But when I began eating normal amounts of food, my mind began working better. I had incredible energy levels. With my new concept of individuality and identity, I was experiencing freedom and I was full of aspirations. I felt alive for the first time in my life.

At first, I was seeing therapists twice a week to keep myself on track. I had a therapy session as well as a session with my dietician every week for a few months. When I felt comfortable, we began decreasing the amount of sessions slowly. I began going to one session a week, then one every other week, then once a month. I saw my dietician once a month for years. She knew me very well, she was the first specialist I'd seen when I was 17.

Getting out of treatment, I had a lot of challenges in front of me. I had to develop my new identity without an eating disorder, outside of treatment. I had to do this without the 24 hour support. This terrified me because I had never lived out on my own, without an eating disorder. I was accustomed to having company, as I'd been in treatment for three months. I wanted to begin identifying myself as "in recovery" instead of anorexic or bulimic.

The appeal of the eating disorder began to dissipate as I grew into my new life.

I AM LEARNING MY WAY IN THIS NEW WORLD

Learning to grocery shop

Grocery shopping was an incredible battle and a beautiful learning curve. In the years before treatment, the only foods I bought in stores were 'negative calorie', or binge food for purging. I had to enter stores with the intention of nourishing my body. I had to make peace with shopping for my well-being. I had to learn how to shop with the knowledge that all of the food would be staying in my stomach.

In the past, I would stare at labels for what seemed like hours. This was a pattern that had turned into a habit. If I intended to keep the food in my stomach, I would stand, obsessing over labels in the grocery store-praying no one was watching me. I would walk up and down aisles, panicking, my mind racing, and walk out empty handed because making decisions about food was paralyzing.

After treatment, I knew that looking at labels would trigger racing thoughts and lead me back to my obsessions and into old patterns and destructive behaviors. I embarked on grocery shopping 'adventures' in which I would buy food that looked and sounded good. I would danger-ously place items in my cart without obsessing over calorie counts and ingredients. I put immense effort into buying groceries that would allow me to put together balanced meals for myself. I chose to make it an ad-venture, instead of a chore. I chose to trust myself and my decisions.

I never look at labels. To this day, I know I cannot, and will not, read calorie counts, sugars, or any other number on a Nutrition Fact label. I avoid looking at calorie counts in restaurant menus- which proves to be difficult sometimes, as they are in huge lettering. If I do happen to glimpse these numbers, I do not make my food choices based on these numbers.

When I was first out of treatment, I vividly remember being terrified of having food in the house. I didn't trust myself not to binge. I dug deep to find the confidence in myself and learned to trust myself and my recovery. Sometimes this was as simple as just going through the motions. Taking action, physically placing items in the cart. Just doing it, not questioning or obsessing.

On my first grocery adventure, I bought a container of peanut butter filled pretzels. I remember the freedom I felt from just placing the container in my cart. I didn't even look at the label. I trusted myself to eat them responsibly. I knew I would enjoy them no matter what their calorie count was. I trusted the pretzels to be fuel for my body. I truly believed that this was a nutritious snack and there was nothing wrong with eating peanut butter pretzels. I bravely ignored a lifetime of my mother's disapproving glances. I squashed my eating disorder's shaming voice. I placed the snack in my cart. It took all of my courage, and faith in the motions, but I purchased them and enjoyed them without my eating disorder.

I HAPPILY NOURISH MY BODY
AND RECEIVE SATISFACTION FROM DAILY MEALS

Staying mindful in daily life

My successful discharge required me to always be *in the moment*. To me, being *in the moment* means acknowledging myself, and all my emotions, in the present moment. It means paying close attention to how I interpret the world around me, and how I handle these emotions. Because the eating disorder was a way for me to numb myself in challenging situations, I had a habit of relying on eating disordered behaviors, and thoughts to focus on, instead of dealing with the challenges in front of me. It was a way for me to disguise my emotions and not deal with anything too 'hard'. I could just focus on the monster in my head that needed tending to.

Being *in the moment* is also referred to as mindfulness. Mindfulness is exactly what it sounds like- keeping my mind full of the present moment. In the past I had come to rely on 'zoning out' mentally by bingeing and purging, focusing on restricting, or overexercising to distract myself with those behaviors instead of dealing with challenging situations in my surroundings. I had to awaken myself and practice bringing my full attention to whatever I was doing. This allowed me to have unique experiences. I began actually experiencing the world around me as opposed to hiding from it. I committed to observing the world around me and began having legitimate experiences. I began allowing my real personality, opinions, and emotions to emanate outward. I began paying close attention to my life and experiencing moments as they happened. It wasn't easy. Sometimes, it was extremely painful, but I learned how to breathe and deal with issues on the spot. I began to uncover a feeling of being alive that I had never experienced before. By having the courage to attend to the present moment, whether it be good or bad, I began to feel connected to the world around me.

Staying connected to my body, my soul, and the events and people around me keeps me from going back into a land of self destruction. Staying mindful helps me appreciate beauty in myself and the world around me. I am able to apply mindfulness to every aspect of my life: my eating habits, my relationships, my employment, and my athletics. I pay attention and fill my mind with taste, texture, smell, hunger level.

Every time I was able to stay in the moment and not drift off into a self-destructive state of mind, the eating disorder lost power over me. My eating disorder hated me for being mindful. It hated the fact that, while I was eating, I was paying attention to taste and fullness level instead of dropping into a zoned-out mindset that would lead me to binge and purge. Or be so overcome with thoughts of guilt, and needing to restrict, that I didn't pay attention to what was going on around me. My eating disorder hated thoughts regarding hunger level and heightened self awareness during meal times. My eating disorder despised that I stayed in the present moment and began accepting each moment for what it was. It hated that I would send warm, appreciative thoughts to my body. My mind became full of what was occurring in my life, as opposed to being preoccupied with the eating disorder and it's commands.

My relationships changed because when I am *in the moment*, committed to staying present, I am aware of my feelings, my state of mind, and how I am processing any given situation. I listen to what people are saying and I respond. I am able to have meaningful conversations with others. I laugh out loud, I cry when I need to. I am authentic and true to myself. I know how I feel and know how to express it in the moment, tactfully, so I do not let myself down, but am gracious with those around me. I no longer let emotions fester, because I am aware and unwilling to postpone hard conversations. Mindfulness in relationships takes a lot of courage, but has been equally rewarding. I know when I am acting authentically and behaving in line with my core values. This has developed over years of not allowing the eating disorder to take control of my every move.

Practicing mindfulness helped me notice and ride the waves of urges when they surfaced. Instead of using the urge to mute the world around me and descend into a self destructive mindset, I acknowledged the urges, without giving in to them. I would pause, and think back a few moments and try to discover where the urge came from. This is called a behavior chain- which behaviors and/or thoughts lead to urges? Usually my urges stemmed from a repressed emotion that I wasn't allowing myself to experience. I committed to being mindful of these urges instead of giving in to them. I became insatiably curious about my state of mind and my behavior chains. It is easy to fall back on old habits and into familiar patterns, but staying mindful required much more energy, patience, and courage.

While I became an expert at analyzing my behavior chains, I also failed many times. Let me repeat that. I failed many times. But being mindful meant being analytical and curious instead of judgemental and harsh for my regression. After engaging in old behaviors, the most important thing I did was accept, without judgement, that relapse happens, and no one is perfect in their recovery.

I EMBRACE MY FLAWS,
KNOWING NOBODY IS PERFECT

Learning from relapse

I have the controversial opinion that in order to recover, you have to relapse. You have to fall hard, many times, and keep getting up to fight. In these moments, we learn how to fight harder or avoid the fall next time

While relapsing, the eating disorder attacked me in many ways. First of all, as with any addiction, the more I engaged in the behaviors the more powerful the thoughts would grow. Acting on the urges, engaging in the eating disorder, gave back the power I worked so hard to take away from it. The eating disorder would be dormant for a bit, I'd have no urges, but it was always waiting around a corner, waiting for a moment of weakness, waiting to strike. These moments were most frequently when I was presented with a stressful situation that I didn't want to confront. My eating disorder was right there to provide me with a distraction, a way out. The urges to engage in the behaviors would be so strong it felt as though the eating disorder was the only option. When I engaged in the behaviors, they became stronger and harder to fight the next time. If I fought hard, the urge would eventually subside and the next time it surfaced, it would be easier to fight. Every time I successfully fought an urge, the next one would be easier to fight, then the next would be even easier, and so on until they barely surfaced anymore.

When I relapsed, the eating disorder would also latch onto the 'All or Nothing' thinking pattern. This led me to be extremely harsh with myself for not being perfect in my recovery. The eating disorder always wanted me to be perfect at everything, and if I couldn't be perfect, why even try? I'd be wracked with guilt and self-doubt, questioning why I was even trying to make recovery oriented decisions when I knew I would just go crawling back to the eating disorder. The eating disorder played this mind-game with me every time I relapsed. The eating disorder would regain power in this vortex. The overpowering, self destructive thinking would lead to the behaviors.

When I relapsed, the eating disorder would punish me for not being perfect. To escape the feelings of imperfection, I'd permit myself to release my mindfulness. In turn, I would allow myself to engage in the behaviors. And the eating disorder would gain a little more power over me. The more I engaged in the behaviors, the stronger the eating disorder would become. The urges would become stronger the next time as well.

This spiral was extremely important for me to witness, experience, and begin to unravel. In order to escape, I had to realize and define exactly what was going on.

I gave myself permission to be imperfect in my recovery. I was able to succeed more because I didn't give up after every failure. Instead of living my life by the mantra, "if you can't do it perfectly, don't do it at all," I began picking myself after my relapses and continuing down the path of recovery. Once I gave myself unconditional permission to mess up, the perfectionist inside me lost power. The perfectionist and the eating disorder worked closely to keep control of me, therefore, denying power to one took power away from both. I continued to remind myself that I didn't need to be perfect, that I am human and I have slip-ups. I had to keep reminding myself that the eating disorder had been a huge piece of my life and I began forgiving myself for being so attached to it.

If I ate dinner and felt I'd eaten too much, I'd feel the need to purge. If I gave in to this urge and acted on it, I tried to forgive myself and tried not to give up for the day. I tried to run my own interventions and stop myself from engaging in a full blown episode of bingeing and purging for the rest of the night because I had "already messed it up for the day." I acknowledged my set-back, analyzed a behavior chain, and fought the urges as hard as I could for the rest of the day.

I wouldn't change any piece of my recovery process, including every single relapse. By relapsing, I was able to learn how to deal with, and cope with, the relapses as they happened. I learned so much about myself and my recovery process through my relapses. I became curious about why they occurred. I began labeling them as learning experiences instead of relapses. While in these learning experiences, I found a new awareness of exactly how my eating disorder operates in my mind and learned how to deal with every little piece.

I remember fighting the urges. Instead of feeling helpless, I became curious. Sometimes the urges were so strong that I felt like the only thing I knew how to do was engage in the behavior, like a robot programmed only for eating disorder behavior. I wanted to conquer these urges. I didn't want temporary fixes or temporary distractions. I wanted to know why they were there, what was causing them, and most importantly, how I could deal with them better the next time.

I worked on identifying and recognizing urges. I was able to identify the emotions that led to the urges and instead of trying to lose myself in the eating disorder, I tried to process the emotion. When I relapsed, I tried not to label myself as 'relapsing'. My eating disorder always gained power from being the "sick one", needing help, and having an excuse to not be the best. I relied on being 'sick', so I had an excuse for my imperfections. While in recovery, I avoided labeling myself as struggling or relapsing because I believe it gave the eating disorder power. I would take my urges and behaviors, and observe them with objective reality, instead of getting sucked back into the vortex. I would force myself to pause, take a breath, and look back at the behavior I had just engaged in. In order to not regress to being the weak, helpless victim, I would allow my relapses to be labeled as learning experiences, not failures. Instead of beating myself up for failing at recovery, I looked at the situation objectively, and traced my steps back to discover what led to the desperation to engage in the behavior in the first place.

I connected all of these recovery oriented behaviors together and I created a structure for myself to rely on when I felt triggered. When I felt the desire to regress to the eating disorder, I kept solidifying my commitment to mindfulness and used this structure to distance myself from the eating disorder.

The perfectionist in me never wanted to admit that I wasn't perfect in my recovery. My objective reality allowed each of these experiences, each of these relapses, to be a chance to learn.

Even years after my discharge from residential treatment, I was continuing to engage in eating disordered behaviors. I struggled with bingeing and purging so severely that my therapist was worried I was regressing to the point I had reached before the Center. It took years of mindfulness out of treatment to completely understand where the urges were coming from and practice making different, more recovery oriented decisions. Every time I gave in, the eating disorder would gain power. I feared terribly that these behaviors would lead me back to where I was before going into treatment.

The urges stemmed from boredom, loneliness, anger, stress, and depression. If I chose to deal with these emotions and not engage in the eating disorder, it meant I had to get really uncomfortable and vulnerable. Over time, I developed solid coping skills to deal with this level of discomfort.

Another pattern that surfaced in my recovery and relapses was what I call "The Last Supper" or the "just this one last time" syndrome. The eating disorder would bargain with me, "just give me this one last time and I'll never do it again." But the more I engaged in the eating disorder, the more I indulged these thoughts, the harder it became to fight. The "Last Supper" refers to the next phase of the cycle: the full blown overindulgence in the behaviors all while thinking, "this is the last time, I swear, I will not do this tomorrow." Sometimes, after just one slip-up, I'd indulge fully in the eating disorder by bingeing and purging and relying on old, familiar behaviors to get me through the discomfort.

There were many nights of unbearable discomfort, living with food in my stomach, bravely staying mindful of my eating, observing my patterns, and accepting where I was in my recovery. The hardest times for me were evenings, when I was bored, alone in my house. I had explored my boredom and knew that it stemmed from a feeling of worthlessness, and without distractions from the day, my old patterns would surface. If I was bored and had food in my stomach, I desired emptiness. I had many evenings where I would eat a normal, healthy dinner with no plans to purge, and ended up sitting through the discomfort, regulating the painful urges to purge and get me back to the familiar place where I could soothe the voices in my head.

I fought hard. I addressed my boredom and loneliness by calling friends, writing letters, or in journals, coloring in coloring books, and reading. Even if I was just staring at a page of words, not really reading at all because my mind was racing with eating disordered thoughts, I was pretending to read. I was occupying my time with normal behaviors, creating new habits, and replacing the eating disorder with real activities. All of these behaviors were real; reading, knitting, coloring, calling friends, taking baths. Through these seemingly negligible activities, I was teaching myself how to experience my life without an eating disorder. I used these activities to distract me, but also as a way to create a real life without the eating disorder.

It took an incredible amount of will-power and strength to give my body what it needed and deserved, but it has been worth it. The less I engaged in the behaviors, the weaker they became, day by day, until they went away. I wanted recovery so badly. I wanted it and I fought for it. It got a little easier everyday.

No one can make me a victim unless I allow them to

Recognizing and working through triggers

Part of learning through relapse was recognizing triggers. Triggers are events, or situations that give rise to, or increase, eating disordered thoughts or behaviors. I had to begin recognizing triggers without acting on them. I was often triggered by comments people made. These were always off-handed comments, completely benevolent in intent, but because I see the world through the filter of the eating disorder, I would be triggered. I'd interpret simple comments like, "Enjoying that sandwich?" As, "You really shouldn't be eating that sandwich, you're fat enough as it is." If someone asked me if I was hungry, I would assume they were asking me because I looked like I ate a lot and must always be hungry. Any comment about food or my body, would go through the filter and be translated into a way for the eating disorder to regain power over me. I had to recognize these as triggers and not allow the eating disorder to sneak back in. I had to hear those misinterpretations as the voice of the eating disorder, not my own.

When I was triggered, and eating disordered thoughts were on the rise, I had to keep making recovery oriented decisions and take action. For example, it would have been much easier for me to stop eating, but I forced myself to keep eating the sandwich. I had to keep paying attention to my hunger levels. I had to keep grocery shopping. Even when I was triggered and my eating disorder was telling me how fat I was, I had to recognise and regulate these thoughts, and continue to eat what I knew I needed to for the day. I kept reminding myself of the difference between my eating disorder and my objective reality.

One of my more challenging triggers is people's comments. The most common, most intense trigger for me is when I mention that I have an eating disorder. Most people say, "Well, you look fine." Or, "Well, you look healthy." This is triggering to me because my eating disorder translates "healthy" as "fat". My eating disorder wanted me to be underweight, and painfully thin. I didn't want to look fine, normal, or healthy.

When these intense triggers got my mind and thoughts racing, I had to rely on my objective reality and continue to convince myself that "healthy" does not mean "fat". Healthy means beautiful. Healthy means I do not have bags under my eyes. Healthy means my hair isn't falling out. Healthy means my nails aren't peeling off in layers. Healthy means I have the energy to engage in activities that bring me joy. Healthy means glowing and nourished, and I look like I take good care of myself.

These comments were triggering because a part of me still wanted to identify with being bulimic or anorexic. If I looked "fine", I wasn't doing a good enough job with my eating disorder. If I looked "fine," I wasn't sick enough and I wasn't getting attention for losing weight. I began trying to detach myself from the desire to identify with the eating disorder. I started to explore other aspects of my personality. I started trying to identify with recovery and with health.

I developed the ability to pause in a situation that felt "icky" and discern when eating disordered thoughts came creeping back in. When situations triggered me, I gave myself permission to pause and take a few moments to figure out what my real motivation was. I'd ask myself why I was doing something, who I was trying to impress, what was the purpose, and what was I trying to accomplish. If it was not a priority for me and my recovery, I knew I had stepped outside the center of my integrity. If my actions were motivated by trying to pacify someone's view of me, or to calm someone else down, I knew I needed to take a step back and remove myself from the situation. If someone's opinion of me is making me step away from my core values, I need to take a moment to reevaluate my actions. I practiced staying in the center of my integrity, firm in my boundaries, and being honest with myself in my recovery. This meant eating when I knew I was supposed to eat, no matter what was going on around me. This meant ignoring all the excuses the eating disorder was fabricating to keep me from eating. It meant standing up for myself and staying authentic to the personality I discovered without the eating disorder. It meant verbalizing my needs in order to take care of myself. It meant staying authentic and trusting that I would be accepted, that I am worthy, just the way I am.

I AM CURIOUS & EAGER TO TRY NEW THINGS

Developing a new identity

The most surprising thing I noticed after discharge was discovering that the eating disorder had ruled every piece of my life. It ruled every decision, everywhere I went, everything I did, and how I felt about it. As I began freeing myself from it, I found the power to develop an entirely new identity without it. My first few months out of treatment, I had no idea what to do with myself. I had never experienced a life without an eating disorder before and I no longer relied on it to make all my decisions for me.

Now, I was in charge, and it was very exciting. Everything I did was based on my own desires, not the eating disorder's. It was unbelievably liberating. I was learning to live all over again. I went out with my friends, and I met new people. I spent time with my family. I made my own decisions about work and mindfully engaged in real life activities. While it was all very exciting, it was very challenging. I had to have a willingness to recover. I had to have the willingness to go to the grocery store, continue to make recovery minded decisions, and put effort into my recovery. I wasn't being monitored 24/7 and I actively had to participate in my new life.

The world without an eating disorder continues to be exciting for me, because I get to create my life and my reality. I get to make it happen based on a beautiful, wholesome, new identity.

I learned to enjoy my own company. I learned what I find pleasurable and what brings me joy. I give myself permission to try new things, knowing that I may not be good at them. I engage in activities that bring me joy, even if I cannot do them perfectly.

I began experiencing emotions, relationships, and connections with people. I began enjoying simple moments. I discovered new ways to function without the eating disorder. Because I was creating a new identity, it was tough at times. But it continued to be fun and surprising. I was an entirely new, mature person, no longer ruled by an eating disorder.

I became excellent at setting boundaries in order to prioritize my recovery. This is just a way of life now, it became a habit to prioritize my recovery. For example, I knew I had to eat at specific times of day so I verbalized this with my friends and family. I informed them that I ate at 8:30a, 12:30p, and 6:30p. At first, I was extremely rigid about the timing of the meals, and it was necessary. I ate at these times, no matter what was going on or where I was. Once I became accustomed to the schedule and took responsibility for not skipping meals, I was able to relax the schedule a little bit at a time. It was important for me to express this boundary, this schedule, with my family, so they could be supportive and helpful in my recovery.

Setting these boundaries, and being explicit with my support system was important so they knew how they could be most helpful. Along with this I asked for emotional space in my recovery. I needed to develop and own my own recovery process. I didn't want to have to share it with everyone. I continued to need things that were my own, and I was terrified that if I began to struggle, my support system would begin to smother me.

I defined this as my Recovery Lifeboat. I imagined my recovery process as a lifeboat that I was on, staying afloat, paddling to shore. If everyone tried to get on my boat, it would sink immediately. Having this image of a boat helped immensely in setting the boundary and letting my support system know that I needed space to recover on my own. My recovery was mine, I was responsible for it, and I would reach out if/when I needed help. This was extremely challenging for my family, as they didn't want me to struggle anymore, they wanted to fix me. They had to trust that I would continue making recovery oriented decisions on my own, they had to trust me unconditionally. I had to go through the actions on my own, knowing that I could reach out if I needed. I am very glad that they gave me my space. My fear was that if I felt like someone was commandeering my lifeboat, I would feel the need to isolate, and shut down. This would have led me back into eating disordered behaviors.

This helped me internalize that I didn't have to share everything with my family. I grew up in a home with very few boundaries, and I needed my space to develop my identity without constantly needing my family's approval.

I HAVE FAITH IN MY PROCESS OF RECOVERY

Staying on track

A happy accident that I believe was a crucial part of my recovery was creating a recovery minded space, home, for myself upon discharge. I created a haven for my recovery. I had a home where I could meditate, a place where I could practice being alone. I had a safe place where I could eat and be grateful for the nutrients. I was in a safe place. I was away from my family and I had a home to return to after a day of reinventing myself. It was as though I had my own treatment center away from CHS. I made a space where I could care for myself outside of treatment, a place where I could practice everything I had learned. I was able to carry all the values I'd learned into the outside world. I surrounded myself with all of the artwork I made during treatment. My placemat that I had made, that was covered in positive affirmations regarding eating and body image, was placed on my dinner table. My entire life revolved around recovery for months. Everything I did was based on recovery. Including how I structured my time. I built time for myself to heal.

I knew that I could not go back to living in my mom's house, the home where my eating disorder started. That was the home that I had engaged in my eating disorder every day since I was 14. It would be too triggering to try to exist in that place without my eating disordered behaviors. I found a new home where I could exist without being haunted by my past triggers. A home where I could reinvent myself without trying to exist where my eating disorder originated. I made a commitment to myself not to engage in the eating disorder within my new, beautiful home.

Another deal I made with myself is that my recovery comes first. My recovery is my number one priority. This is a deal that I have been able to uphold with myself, to this day. My recovery is my top priority, because nothing else can exist without a solid recovery. I prioritize my recovery over my employment, my education, my career, and my relationships. It sounds harsh and overly rigid, but nothing else exists in my life without my recovery. I take care of myself and my recovery before anything else in my life, and everything falls into place afterward. I continue to make recovery oriented decisions and enjoy a life that is not dictated by the size of my body.

I NEED NEVER GO BACK AGAIN

Stopping the behaviors

The best commitment I made in regards to my recovery was to stay off of scales. I cannot regulate the emotions that come along with having a number attached to my body. The latent eating disorder would latch on to the number no matter what. If the number was too high I would be triggered to start losing weight. If the number is lower than I expected, I would begin to challenge myself to get it even lower. I will never allow myself to engage in this game again. Even now, over ten years in recovery, I know it would be dangerous for me to know my weight. I absolutely will not step on a scale. And I have had to fight with actual people (not just my eating disordered thoughts) to maintain this boundary.

When I first got out of treatment and knew I had to maintain this pact with myself, I refused to get weighed at the doctor's office. Before I knew the proper terminology, this led to many disagreements with nurses. I would say, "Can we skip the scale today?" It was usually met with a shrug and an apathetic, "Ok".

But once it was met with an argumentative, "We haven't weighed you in over a year, the doctor needs to know your weight."

I replied, "I have a history with a very severe eating disorder and it's dangerous for me, I'd like to skip the scale."

This nurse rolled her eyes, and said, "Bitch." As she walked out of the room.

I did not care about the name calling, I stood by my boundaries. I know myself, I know my triggers and even stepping on a scale, knowing someone somewhere had a number attached to my body, this was all extremely dangerous for me. Even the sound of the scale was triggering. I know that I am an addict when it comes to numbers associated with my body. It would be like giving a recovered alcoholic a glass of wine and expecting it to not be a big deal. As much as I wish I wouldn't, I know that if my weight was written down somewhere I would find myself "stumbling across it".

I discussed this with my general practitioner who was appalled at the nurses behavior. She agreed with me, that they do not need to weigh me, that as long as my therapist was occasionally taking my weight in a safe environment, there was simply no need. She put a note in my file that says, "DO NOT WEIGH PATIENT." And gave me the verbiage to refuse the scale.

From that moment forward I can say, "Can we skip the scale?" If that is met with any disagreement, I can say, "It should say in my file DO NOT WEIGHT PATIENT." At this point the nurses usually apologize and move on. In the 10 years since, I have only had to escalate this once. The next step is to "refuse the procedure." If the nurses continue to fight with me about getting on the scale, I simply say, "Please write that the patient is refusing the procedure."

This seems like a lot of battles, a lot of work, almost overkill to protect myself, but I am glad for every single step I have taken to uphold my boundaries. I know that scales are triggering. I know that the sound, the feeling, the knowledge that someone has my weight written down, this is all detrimental to my healing and I have figured out ways to protect myself.

I made many commitments, and pacts, with myself to try to keep myself on track. One of these was, out of respect for the owners of the home I was living in, I would not engage in my eating disorder in the house. This led me to bingeing and purging in my car in empty parking lots (while struggling in relapse), which was frighteningly similar to my behaviors before treatment. I continued to see my therapist, and was honest about my relapses. I could tell she was worried, but never judgemental.

When in one of these episodes, I would buy binge food, drive to a parking lot outside of a casino (since no one thought my behavior was odd there) and proceed to binge and purge over the course of about an hour, and then drive home. This became a spot of mine. I went there a couple more times over the next few weeks. Since I refused to engage in my behavior in the house, this led me to drive to parking lots and engage in behaviors there. Anyone who has dealt with an addiction understands this behavior. I knew it was dangerous, but I continued to do it regardless.

This continued until Halloween, when I attended a party inside the casino of one of my parking lot binge/purge spots. I went to the party dressed as a tree, "Mother Nature", and I met a Lumber Jack on the dance floor. We connected immediately. This man would eventually teach me more about myself than any one person ever had. He would teach me how to stand up for myself, how to set boundaries with people you love, and what I deserve out of a relationship. Not because he was all of these things, but because he wasn't. Our relationship and interactions taught me that I am more capable than I ever gave myself credit for.

I fell in love with the Lumber Jack the moment I met him. We went outside to his car, in the parking lot, where I met his dog. We chatted and played fetch for hours. Out of respect for that moment, and that night, I stopped bingeing and purging there in that parking lot. The places where I could engage in my behaviors were getting few and far between. It was becoming a huge inconvenience to indulge my urges.

One day, I had an experience that placed an entirely new light on what I was doing to my body and how badly it needed to stop. The morning after New Year's Eve, I was hung-over and feeling miserable from the night before. I ran to the bathroom and knelt with my head in the toilet, throwing up *involuntarily*. I dry-heaved until I was throwing up bile. And it hurt. I tasted the bile making my teeth sticky and had to hold the sides of the toilet as I felt like someone was punching me in the gut trying to get the toxins out of my body. I realized that this is throwing up. It was out of control and extremely painful. It hurt my throat, my stomach, my mouth.

The experience of forcing myself to throw up versus actually throwing up because my body needed it were vastly different. Purging was always a method for me to feel in control, a way to gain my power back. Purging rarely even hurt anymore. It was just an emotional, physical release that my body craved. But throwing up for real was wildly out of control and extraordinarily painful.

I put the pieces together that the purging I engaged in regularly was giving me the *illusion of control*. That throwing up was hard on the body and I never wanted to put my body through that again. Reminding myself that purging was an *illusion of control* and that throwing up is wildly out of control helped me put my behaviors back into perspective. Purging was no longer an option. The first few days after the hangover I didn't even have any urges, because the physical memory of throwing up was still in my body. But the agreement to not purge proved difficult, sometimes I felt it was impossible, many times over the next several months.

I was committed to never throwing up again. I was committed to many nights of discomfort and writhing through urges. I knew that I would not gain control of a situation or prove anything by putting my body through the wringer anymore.

Every day that I fought through the urges, they became less and less powerful. I was, once again, gaining my personal power back from the eating disorder. No one was monitoring my bathroom visits, no one was keeping track of me for 30 minutes after every meal. I felt empowered, I was doing it on my own and the eating disorder was losing power everyday.

My eating disorder was chaos. It made decisions to sabotage me, all while tricking me into believing it was the best decision. I thought it was looking out for my best interest. But my authentic self nurtures me and takes care of my body and soul. It makes the best decisions for my longevity, and acts out of love for me as a whole being.

I MOVE BEYOND MY OLD LIMITATIONS AND ALLOW MYSELF TO EXPRESS FREELY AND CREATIVELY

Introducing meat into my diet

After being out of residential treatment for over a year, I decided to start eating meat. I had been a vegetarian for almost 15 years- except for the time my family went on a no-carb diet. Like many of the others, this diet didn't last long, it was just another on the list I embarked on as an adolescent.

I didn't know it at the time, but beginning to eat meat became another important piece of my recovery. I realized that I didn't even know why I was a vegetarian. For a while, I claimed it was ethical reasons, which made sense, but it wasn't exactly true. I began to realize that vegetarianism was the very first form of restricting I engaged in. It was the first way I learned how to control what I was eating, from a very young age. It was a way to control, a way to cut out an entire food group, even when I was eight years old. It was my first practice in refusing food, and making up excuses not to eat at birthday parties, at BBQ's, or picnics. The main course was usually meat, so I had found an easy way to refuse food.

This was an incredible discovery because I was able to clearly see that my eating disorder had been using vegetarianism to control me from a very young age. Eating meat meant I no longer had obvious excuses to refuse food at public events. It meant I had a new food group to explore, it meant I was letting go of one more diet and taking back one more way the eating disorder controlled me. As frightening as it was to let go of the rigid rules regarding meat, I allowed myself to become adventurous in exploring new foods. I called it my Meat Venture, and I learned how to cook and taste all kinds of meat.

At first, I was terrified of eating meat, but I couldn't figure out why. It came back to control, I felt out of control without my rules.

Vegetarianism was the last set of rules I had around food. These rules gave me the structure I craved, these rules gave the eating disorder power. I also used to get attention for my vegetarianism and for restricting. I always felt like I had power over everyone else because I was not eating what everyone else was eating. I had emotions and feelings of control surrounding my vegetarianism. This was just the eating disorder disguised as a 'health-nut'. To take away this control from the eating disorder, I had to begin to eat meat. In the past, I had never associated myself with meat. I never learned to cook it, I avoided it all together. When introducing meat into my life, I took power away from the eating disorder.

After giving up my last frontier of restriction, I could clearly see that vegetarianism was an illusion of control for me and I know that my well-rounded recovery means I cannot be on a diet. If I need to eliminate certain foods due to allergies or preferences, I can, but I no longer allow myself to have any behaviors that even remotely resemble dieting. This includes any type of restriction from any food group. I understand that this is not the case for everyone, but I know that my eating disorder would sneak back in if I decided to stop eating carbohydrates, or go on a 'gluten-free kick'. Many people's brains can handle that type of "dieting", mine cannot.

Everytime I nourished myself, made myself a balanced meal (complete with meat), every time I took care of my needs, I took power away from the eating disorder.

I AM WORTHY OF LOVE

Learning to function in relationships

I learned a lot about my existence without an eating disorder from the Lumber Jack I met at the Halloween party. He helped me recognise a lot about myself, most of it being necessary for my recovery. He was the first person in my life who gave me space to be myself and gave me space to develop and explore everything I am capable of. He encouraged my creative ideas, instead of shooting them down. I felt like he was the first person in my life to accept me exactly as I am, without trying to change me. He appreciated and encouraged every aspect of my personality. Everything. No judgements, just acceptance. I had never experienced that before. He introduced me to new activities, a new way of exercising: activity for fun, weight loss wasn't even in the picture. He was an incredible playmate. In fact, we were outside playing so much, I had to eat way more than I was used to just to be able to maintain the energy level to keep up with all the fun activity. It was all about having fun! We skied, snowboarded, climbed mountains, rode bicycles- all for fun! We inhaled fresh air and I breathed life into my new identity. He loved how much energy I had, and how full of life I was.

I have so much energy because I wake up grateful everyday that I didn't die in the grips of the eating disorder. I know how close to death I was, so when I stand on top of a mountain that I've climbed, it has a significance to me that not everyone understands. Backpacking and skiing have a whole different meaning for me. It's not just backpacking, it's connecting with my body, out in nature, knowing that my body is capable and alive. I lived through a time when it wasn't and I am grateful for every moment and every breath of air I get.

I lived about an hour's drive from the Lumber Jack so we didn't see each other as often as I would have liked, and I felt like when I wasn't around, I fell off his radar. But I was so enamored with him, I found

myself willing to tolerate his lack of commitment and lack of communication, just to be in his company. I wanted to fully enjoy the little time
we got to spend together.

This pattern continued over a period of a few years, and through
this, I learned what I will and will not tolerate in a relationship. I learned
what I deserve and how to speak up and ask for what I need. I learned to
clarify expectations and how to open the lines of communication, even
though it is extremely hard. I learned that I deserve to be with someone
who loves me as much as I love them. I deserve to be with someone who
is thinking about me when I'm not around. I deserve to be communicated with openly and honestly. I no longer tolerate people ignoring my
texts or calls. I deserve to be with someone who supports me in my recovery, in my goals, in my education, in my athletics, and in my
relationships.

After three years with this man, I was whole-heartedly committed
and unconditionally in love. He wavered between commitment to me
and self-absorption. I verbalized all of this and what I want out of a relationship, what I wanted from him. I verbalized my needs, I set
boundaries. Tolerating much less for years made me realize how desperately I wanted to be in a healthy, functional relationship. While in this
relationship I got to practice courageously asking for what I want, knowing what I deserve. We eventually had to break up because I knew he
wouldn't ever be able to give me everything I deserve.

All of this practice was part of figuring out who I am without an
eating disorder. I began figuring out who I am, how I want to live my
life, what I need, what I will tolerate, and how to express these needs so
they do not go unmet. Learning how to express these needs took a while
and a lot of practice. I came up with strategies for learning how to initiate
hard conversations.

The first time I hinted that I'd like to talk about "us", I told him
earlier in the day. I said, "I'm coming over tonight, I'm bringing gin &
tonics, and we are having a conversation about this relationship." He was
so surprised by my forwardness, he nodded and responded, "Ok."

But I didn't always want to have hours of lead time, I didn't want to
keep scheduling my emotions like meetings, so I started trying to talk
about our relationship in the moments when I was feeling extreme

emotions (instability, frustration, depression) about it. For exceptionally challenging conversations, that I really wanted to initiate, I would come up with exactly what I wanted to say. I'd rehearse over and over. Then wait for a moment of quiet, and count to three in my head. Like jumping off of a high-dive when I was a kid. If I was scared, I would count to three and jump. So, I held myself responsible, took three seconds to gather my courage and began the conversation. I did this many times. I found relief in being able to have these conversations, but they never went the way I wanted them to. I would express that I needed more commitment, I wanted a label, I wanted to be his girlfriend and be treated accordingly. He would always respond with his desires to stay uncommitted, but that we were such great playmates, "let's just stay buddies."

My relationship status has changed a lot over the past 10 years, but at the point in my life when I met the Lumber Jack, I needed to love someone as much as I had loved the eating disorder. He filled that role, that void, and much more. While trying to recover, the instability in our relationship was the thing that would continually trigger my eating disorder. I had to deal with emotions that came along with being completely in love with someone, and having them not return the feeling. I had to deal with the anger, the loneliness, the sadness, the feelings of unworthiness, and my own indecisiveness in whether I was willing to stop seeing him until he was ready to commit to me or not.

When I was angry with the relationship, I felt full all the time. I hated eating, I hated taking care of myself, and I had to realize that I was full of anger, not food. My emotions were still tricking me into thinking that I didn't need to eat. During these emotionally stressful times, I found it difficult to take basic care of myself; shower, brush my teeth, get out of bed, and most of all, eat. The greatest challenge was that if I skipped a meal, or didn't eat as much as I should, the eating disorder would perceive this as a victory and encourage me to continue skipping meals. I was able to label these as eating disorder thoughts, because they were so familiar and uncomfortable. I would feel my desire to experiment with how long I could go without eating. I felt myself needing the control that I felt when I skipped meals. In highly emotional times, I wanted my body to be empty. I fought these urges, I fought to not let the eating disorder sneak back in using my emotions. I fought to chew and swallow what I knew my body needed even though my eating disorder was screaming at me.

The Lumber Jack and I decided to call it quits for the final time a few years into my recovery process. It was at a time that I felt strong in my recovery, I hadn't purged in over two years, I was no longer struggling with bulimic behaviors, and my therapist had been keeping track of my weight so I knew I had been a consistent weight for years. The Lumber Jack and I had been in and out of a relationship that resembled one of 'friends with benefits' and one side always wanted a more solid commitment. I'd finally had enough of him not treating me with the respect I asked for.

I went into a deep depression. I was heartbroken. I was furious. I was angry that I'd spend years loving someone who couldn't love me back, someone who had taken advantage of my love for years. The eating disorder and the judgemental voices in my head were right there to soothe me. I was no longer using bingeing and purging to cope, but my body, once again became a punching bag to express what I didn't know how to express emotionally. I felt betrayed. I didn't know how to express this extreme disappointment. I began feeling like if I had just been pretty enough, if I had just been nice enough, if I had been fun enough, he would have realized and began to love me the way I loved him. If I had just been more. All of these traits I had associated with being thin. In my state of vulnerability, I began to believe that if I had just been thin enough he would have loved me.

After the final breakup, I began struggling with restriction. I'd eat a healthy breakfast, pack myself a lunch, and sit at work all day trying to find the strength to eat. I'd vacillate between willingness and strength, and complete surrender to the eating disorder. I started losing weight again and this gave even more power back to the eating disorder. I'd go home in the evening, after work, and make myself dinner. But after a bite or two, my eating disorder would convince me that I wasn't hungry and I didn't need it. It would tell me that I'd "*done so good throughout the day,*" that I'd "*eaten so little and eating dinner was unnecessary.*" It would tell me that if I could go through the day without eating, I "*couldn't possibly need dinner.*" The eating disorder would tell me that what I made for dinner wasn't appetizing anyways, that it was gross, and wouldn't even taste that good. So why waste my time? My recovery-oriented mind would swoop in and join the battle. It would remind me that

I needed to try to eat, that I needed to fight, that a meal skipped is a battle lost. I'd go back into the kitchen and make something else that sounded more appetizing. Pretty soon, I was surrounded by uneaten food that I was trying to eat. The eating disorder would be telling me that it was unnecessary and gross and I would fight back telling myself that I needed the nourishment, that I had to eat something, anything. Soon, I'd be so exhausted from the battle, that I would drink a glass of wine and go to bed, empty stomach. Losing the battle.

I realized that I was struggling again, this time with restriction. When I had these episodes, these relapses, it usually took me a couple months to notice the pattern and label it. I would get caught up in the "just this last time, I'll be different tomorrow," trap and a couple months would pass before I realized that I was struggling.

This time, I wanted to be hungry. My hunger meant I was losing weight again, that I was changing back into a stick figure. When I went to my therapist she mentioned that I looked scrawny. My eating disorder loved this and thought it was a compliment. I mentioned that I thought I was struggling; that I was having trouble eating and I was thriving off feeling like I was losing weight.

"So, what are you going to do about this?" she asked, pointedly.

"I don't know what to do. I can't eat. But I want to know *why* I've started struggling now."

"Does it have anything to do with being single?"

"I like being single. I don't miss him. I miss the stability. But the relationship was never that stable. I'm mad at him and the way he treated me. If I had just been more, I dunno, something. More fun, prettier, smarter."

"If you'd been thinner?"

"Yeah. Any trait that I can think of, I associate with being skinny. So, yeah, I feel like if I had just been thinner, it would've worked out."

"Are you trying to prove something to him by losing weight?" She asked.

"Yeah, like, if I lost weight I'd get attention from him. All the attention I never got. All the attention I needed."

I was using my body as a way to express something I didn't know how to express. I was going to get skinny, painfully skinny, and he was going to give me attention, all the attention he never gave me, years worth of attention. I was going to lose weight and use my body to get back at him. My eating disorder had me believing that this was completely logical.

"Say you do lose all this weight, and you do get the attention. It's not going to be the loving attention you crave. It's going to be negative, focused on your eating disorder, not on you.

"You are retaliating in anger through weight loss. This is illogical, and unhealthy.

"Years from now, you're going to remember him, you're going to remember the breakup. You will remember being upset, and being depressed, BUT you have the choice right now to make a memory of getting through it, pulling through and coming out stronger on the other side. Stronger than ever. Do not sabotage this opportunity with a full blown relapse."

Once I understood that I was angry and trying to retaliate by starving myself and losing weight, I was able to start winning more and more of the battles. Refusing food was not accomplishing the revenge I so desired. Instead of letting urges overpower me, I began to question them again. I'd ask myself why the urge was there, why did I want to change my body, what was I really trying to accomplish?

The eating disorder seemed to be waiting for my moments of weakness. My moments of weakness were those when I felt the most vulnerable. I've learned that I am very sensitive and sarcastic comments, harsh criticisms, and lack of support trigger my intense emotions. The moments when I am feeling intense anger, frustration, loneliness, shame, or lack of control trigger my eating disordered thoughts. I had to build up emotional recognition and resilience. At first, if I got criticized at work, someone cancelled plans on me, or I felt lonely, these tiny things were ways that the eating disorder would come creeping back in. I became hyper-aware when these emotions existed. It wasn't always me who pointed it out, it was usually my therapist.

I tried to sit in stillness, fighting urges, and listen to my body. This took years and years of practice. Years of trying to listen and not being able to. Years of just going through the motions because I knew it was what I was supposed to do for recovery.

"THE QUESTION ISN'T WHO IS GOING TO LET ME, IT'S WHO IS GOING TO STOP ME" -AYN RAND

The Final Relapse

At many points in those years, I never thought I would recover. I began starting to accept that it would just always be a part of my life. Always waiting for a moment of weakness. I would half-heartedly fight my urges to binge and purge, and occasionally win the battle. I felt that it was just a part of who I was. I could go a couple weeks, even a couple months without engaging in the behaviors, but I still figured my lack of behaviors was temporary.

My last significant relapse lasted over two years. I was struggling with relationships and body image. I had not taken enough time to fully develop the coping skills I needed to process extreme emotions. I drank wine to numb my feelings. I drank a lot. I drank so much one night that it made me sick and I threw up. I hadn't purged in a while, so the emptiness was a huge relief. And I didn't have the guilt associated with purging. I began drinking wine to excess every night in order to make myself sick. The eating disorder had snuck it's way back in and I didn't even realize it. I was free to drink to the point of throwing up and I didn't label it as eating disordered behavior, because I was *actually sick from the alcohol.*

This didn't happen everyday, or even every week, at first. It started with just one instance. Then a second several weeks later. Then a third a few weeks after that. Within 6 months, I was back to bingeing and purging almost everyday, sometimes many times a day, and I didn't think I was ever going to be able to stop. I began hating myself again and accepting that this behavior was just a part of who I was and as long as it didn't get out of control like five years ago, I would be able to live my life this way.

It got worse again to the point when my therapist suggested I go back to the Center. That comment triggered me to begin trying to fight the urges once more. I fought hard, but still felt as though I was losing.

My final weeks in the grips of the eating disordered behaviors were a series of divine intervention, spiritual discoveries, and moments of clarity.

My sister's wedding in October of 2015 was a significant event in the life of my recovery. Weddings are stressful. Even if you are not the one getting married, even if your family gets along, even if there is no underlying drama. Weddings are stressful. The entire family would be there, I was the only bridesmaid, so I would need to look good in my dress. I was single. I felt I had nothing to brag about while making small talk with family, the new in-laws, and friends. Everything about that wedding made me feel like a very little sister again, a very unsuccessful little sister.

I didn't even attempt to fight the eating disorder that weekend. I let it drive the train, completely in control, and I just obeyed. Part way through that weekend I was conversing with my mother's partner about the stress and how it was affecting me. My mother's partner is a recovered alcoholic and truly understands the experience of an addiction. I felt safe telling her that I wasn't even struggling, I wasn't fighting, I was just indulging in the eating disorder that weekend.

"I think it's unreasonable to ask me to get through this weekend, this stress, all the family stuff, and everything *without* an eating disorder." I looked at her, completely numb, and she nodded.

"Yeah, I get it. Makes sense to me."

I verbalized that I was blatantly engaging in the behaviors as a coping mechanism. I was admitting that I had no better way to cope. And she gave me permission to do so. In that moment, it was perfectly clear to me how I had been using the eating disorder my whole life. I had been waiting for that moment of clarity. I had been trying to find a perfectly clear example of a time where I needed coping skills, why I should develop coping mechanisms, and be able to regulate my emotions. Up until that moment, that weekend, the weekend of the wedding, I had yet to clearly see how my eating disorder had functioned for me for so many years. While I understood it at a superficial level, I didn't fully comprehend it until I was *given permission* to use it to get me through a stressful event.

"I think it's unreasonable to ask me to get through this weekend… without my eating disorder."

I couldn't believe those words had come out of my mouth. I heard them come out and have never forgotten what it sounded like. I wasn't even overcome with the "Last Supper" syndrome. I knew I would engage in the behaviors to get me through the weekend, I did not know that this sudden clarity would be the catalyst for the urges to begin dissipating.

A few weeks before the wedding, I began using an app on my iphone to track my behaviors and emotions. It was an app targeted specifically for eating disorders. I tracked my eating patterns every day. After a few weeks, it could graph my emotions, my behaviors, and my eating patterns and display perfectly clear behavior chains. I had the data to help me begin breaking these behavior chains. I wished I had started using this app much earlier. It provided perfect clarity, instead of just the information existing in my head. The data could show me the exact cause of what led me to engage in the behaviors.

About a month after the wedding, I went with my mom to visit my grandpa who was on hospice and declining quickly. We changed his shirt, wiped out his mouth, put lotion on his hands, and I was overwhelmed with a feeling that I labeled as selfishness at the time. I couldn't believe that I had spent the majority of my life seeking my grandparents' approval. I couldn't believe I had designed my life to please these people and here he was dying. He was going to die and I would be stuck with the life that I created for my grandparents', and my mother's, validation. I would be stuck.

I began looking at everything I did in my life; my job, my activities, and did an audit of what I did for myself and what I did to please my family. I gave myself freedom and permission to begin designing my life the way I wanted it, not designing it to impress my family. This began my new lifelong path of self discovery based on truly getting in touch with my desires and motivations. In my moment of perceived selfishness, I untangled another level of the eating disorder.

Another moment of divine clarity in those few weeks that led to the eating disorder really losing its power over me, was mid-November 2015. My parents had to put their cat to sleep. His health had been declining for years and the vet came to their house to euthanize him. As we sat with him in the days leading up to his release, in deep meditation, I heard this cat tell me that he would take anything from me that I no longer needed. He would take it with him when he died and release it into the universe.

I asked him to take away my eating disorder. That it was no longer serving me. It had functioned for me for almost 15 years and it had served me well. But now that I could see exactly why I needed it, I was compelled to shed it, and really grow into a woman who had the courage to regulate emotions and deal with her life. I truly believe this cat, Boo, took what was left of the urges with him when he passed.

After all my battles in the years following treatment, these few moments in the fall of 2015 led to the eating disorder finally, completely losing its power over me. I clearly saw where I needed to develop new skills, a new life, new coping mechanisms, and I committed.

It was serendipitous that at the end of such a long, fierce battle, the events lined up perfectly for me to stop engaging in the behaviors, and a cat took my eating disorder away. I have always been and will continue to be a very spiritual person, and I am grateful everyday that these events lined up the way they did for me. The app, the wedding, my grandpa's decline, and the cat's death. I did the homework, I had been preparing myself for this release all along. I was able to capitalize on these moments because I had been preparing myself for them, and for the opportunity to finally release my eating disorder.

The urges lost power over me. The urges were no longer debilitating, they became manageable. I was truly exploring and seeing their function, and they no longer had power over me. I was free.

REMEMBER YOU ONCE DREAMED
OF BEING WHO YOU ARE NOW

Advanced Recovery

I've spent the past five years in what I refer to as Advanced Recovery. I am no longer engaging in eating disordered behaviors, but the thoughts are still there, though few and far between. I will go for days, sometimes weeks at a time without having eating disordered thoughts. At first, the urges were strong, but when I didn't engage in them, didn't indulge in bingeing and purging or restricting, they dissipated over time. Once I was not occupied with fighting urges, the thoughts began to dissipate as well. I could distinguish them from my own clear headed thoughts and behave in a self nurturing way.

Over the months and eventually years, the thoughts were so few and far between that when I did get triggered, it would blindside me. I recognized it immediately and would stop whatever I was doing and work through the trigger. Let me repeat that, *I stopped what I was doing and worked through the trigger.* I would say it out loud, I would figure out what exactly was in the moment that was triggering me. I did not try to ignore it or muscle through it. I did not white knuckle myself through these triggers, I stopped and worked through them.

Every single trigger was an opportunity to learn something new about my Advanced Recovery- something new about myself. I gained power and strength through learning how to deal with these triggers as they surfaced. I would be patient and gentle with myself, and I would grow further into my recovery because of it.

Verbalizing a trigger always helps. Claiming, "I'm really triggered right now," or "that's really triggering because..." has been immensely helpful. It not only helps me sort through my thoughts, but it informs those around me, my support system, how to interact with me.

Journaling, getting the words that are racing in my head, out on paper has been helpful as well. Even when the journal entries are incoherent or streams of consciousness, it gets these debilitating thoughts out of my head and onto paper. Journaling helps me organize my racing thoughts.

Being gentle with myself means knowing when to leave a situation and not force myself through a painful experience. Dealing with triggers is extremely necessary. I refuse to go through my life shielding myself from challenging situations, but I also know when to remove myself and protect myself. Learning how to process triggers is extremely important in Advanced Recovery, as I am not willing to live my life walking on eggshells, trying to appease my latent eating disorder. I want it to rear its ugly head every now and again to help me reach another level in my recovery. To conquer one more trigger, one more challenge.

I have radically accepted that there will be triggers, there will be challenging situations, and it is my choice to learn to deal with them and not relapse. I pause, verbalize my thoughts with those around me, and recenter myself. I take inventory of behaviors, emotions, and make small gentle moves to maneuver my way through the trigger.

Because I am open about my struggles, I am able to have a few relationships in my life with other women who are in Advanced Recovery as well. We are all proud of our history, where we've been and what we've overcome. Our conversations sometimes remind me of my first few days at the Center- when I could verbalize my eating disordered thoughts and was stunned that everyone understood what I was saying. We're able to joke about these thoughts now, in a very healthy way. And support each other, in a loving way, when triggers surface.

While it is nice to have someone who understands, these friendships do not revolve around eating disorder recovery. These are friendships that I would have, with incredible women, regardless. My identity is a strong, powerful woman. I am no longer defined by my struggles or even my recovery. I am completely different and surround myself with individuals who have solid identities as well.

Strange triggers are seemingly everywhere and I use them as opportunities to continue on my path to recovery. Simple things like seeing a calorie count next to an item on a menu or if someone around me is trying to lose weight. Or even worse, won't stop talking about how much weight they've lost. Even ads in my social media feed targeted at healthy living or healthy eating could trigger eating disordered thoughts. I practiced being able to separate myself out from the need to indulge in these thoughts or listen to the voices in my head. When these triggers surface, out of the blue, I regulate and do not entertain the eating disorder's desires.

Along with no longer identifying myself as anorexic, bulimic, struggling, or even in recovery, I am breaking out of the victim mindset. I am continually breaking out of the pattern of being the "sick one." I have begun taking initiative in my life regardless of my past. Regardless of what has happened in my past or what has happened to me, I take responsibility for myself. The challenging piece of this is that I did spend 15 years wrapped up, distracted, and did not properly develop coping skills. My successes look different than those of my peers because of my struggles with my eating disorder. I know how to take care of my depression, my triggers, etc so I do not get sucked under again. I have to truly believe in my successes and be proud of where I've been, while not letting it hold me back from continuing to take on challenges, try new things, etc.

I often struggle with insecurities based on my lack of success compared to my peers. I have been working to let go of my excuses that have to do with depression and my eating disorder history. I have had a habit in the past of using these struggles as an excuse to not push myself or try new things. I recognise when I am letting myself off the hook and using my history as an excuse to not give my best, or do my best. This recognition is very important and a huge step in my advanced recovery.

I have to continually remind myself that my recovery is a success that many people will not understand. I have to be proud of myself and continue to move forward- even if it feels as though I am falling far behind my peers and their accomplishments.

Comparisons are something that I have to be very cognizant about. Especially comparing myself to the updates I see on peers' social media. A few years ago, I made a deal with myself that I would not make decisions or take actions based on FOMO, "Fear of Missing Out." When looking at my Instagram or Facebook feed, I get very intense bouts of FOMO and then feel guilty for not living someone else's life, and then I make decisions that are based on my social media feeds, instead of my own desires- instead of acting from the center of my integrity.

Recognizing this dysfunctional pattern, I chose to observe when I was making decisions based on FOMO or what I truly desired. This practice has helped me in my recovery, in getting in tune with myself, and acting on self-nurturing thoughts, not thoughts driven by what other people are doing. When observing other's lives becomes too intimidating or my sense of FOMO becomes overwhelming, I take the responsibility upon myself to take a break from social media until I get my priorities back in order. I take breaks from social media when I need to prioritize and recenter myself.

I am successful. I accept where I am on any given day. I listen to my body and take care of it. I continue to learn about myself. I continue to explore my personality and everything that I am capable of. This is success.

While I know that humor has been a dysfunctional coping mechanism for me in the past, I have been able to morph it into a functional skill for me to use. This includes being able to joke about my triggers in order to talk about them. For example, when my father was in the hospital a few months prior to his passing, my sister and I went to the house he had been staying at to clean out the refrigerator (we didn't know when he'd be released from the hospital). Everything about this experience was anxiety provoking: a new level of sadness, confusion, and stress that I had never experienced before. As I poured a container of leftover soup into the sink and the garbage disposal I felt myself say out loud, "Wow, I miss throwing up, " and added wistfully, "Aww, bulimia." My sister looked at me and I shrugged. Sometimes I have to say things like this out loud to take power away from the triggers. I laughed at my own joke, knowing that no matter how sad or stressful a situation is, throwing up is no longer an option.

In my journey of Advanced Recovery, I have developed a set of coping mechanisms and skills that help me deal with high stress situations, or even daily stressors, without reverting to unhealthy habits. The most powerful tool I have developed is journaling. I free-flow-write on a daily basis to help me outline, and organize, my thoughts. I write everything from letters to people that I do not intend to send, to gratitude lists, to stream of consciousness, and recording my dreams. Anything and everything that goes through my head gets written down in a journal, because this has been the most effective way for me to identify and process emotions. I have journals and pens stashed everywhere in my home so I'm never without a place to record my thoughts.

Another coping skill I have discovered easing anxiety for me is baths. When I am depressed, I take baths. I put music on and sit in hot water. This eases my anxiety in a few ways. The first is being occupied with sensations. The smells, the feeling of the water, the lighting from the candles, all occupy my mind and I can relax by just focusing on sensations. The other way baths ease my anxiety is unusual. For some reason, baths make me feel like I am "doing something" even when I am depressed and feel like I cannot physically or mentally get anything done. Just this simple act of self-care eases my anxiety, because I am doing something to take care of myself.

A huge mark of progress in my journey of developing coping skills is awareness of my emotional state and being gentle with myself when I am vulnerable, down, hurt, or anxious. Over the years I have learned to pinpoint these emotions and verbalize them. After identifying them, I can act accordingly to take the best care of myself I possibly can. Sometimes it is as simple as taking a bath. Other times, I get a massage and then go home to a nice bottle of wine. Sometimes it takes a bit more effort, like reaching out to my support system to see if anyone can come over for dinner and laugh with me. I have spent the past few years learning who I can go to for which kind of support. I have developed an awareness of who I can reach out to depending on what I need. I listen to my emotions, my body, my intuition, and allow it to inform me of what I need. And then I ask for specific help. I have also learned to recognise when I need alone time to make myself a nice dinner and enjoy my own company. I am able to shamelessly proclaim these needs and take care of them.

Advanced Recovery also includes setting and maintaining good boundaries for myself regarding my relationships and my self-care. I listen to my needs and I take care of myself first. If I'm thirsty, I drink. If I want a piece of chocolate, I buy one and eat it without needing validation from those around me. If I need to put on more sunscreen, I do it. In the past, I would seek validation from those around me in order to take care of my needs. Now, when I'm tired, I take a nap or sit still for a minute. I listen to my body and what it needs, not what others around me assume I need. I have a thorough self care regimen that I take initiative to engage in.

I realize now, that the body image battle may be one I fight for the rest of my life. While the way I see my body no longer dictates my behaviors, my body image is still affected by my emotions. I recognise this and choose to not act on it, or do anything different with food or exercise. I am fascinated by the power of my mind to instantly see flaws on my body when I am under stress. I know that my body hasn't changed at all, it is all in my mind and my imagination, but when I become very anxious or upset, I suddenly feel like my pants are too tight or I see extra layers of fat on my arms. The key to getting through these moments is to not fixate or ruminate about the size of my body. I allow myself to acknowledge the size I see myself, I acknowledge the stressors in my life, and I accept that this interpretation is temporary. I know that the next time I look in a mirror, or similar, I will feel different- perhaps back to normal, perhaps bigger, but I know it is all in my head and I refuse to change my behaviors to try to manipulate my body size.

I engage in playtime (exercise) when I want to, not out of obligation to my eating disorder or body image. Sometimes it's because I want fresh air, sometimes it's because I want to feel my body moving through space, sometimes it's because I want to ski under a full moon, or feel my body cruising on my bike- fast as I can. If I ever feel myself falling into the trap of weight loss or calorie counting thought patterns, I stop, take a deep breath, focus on the birds or other noises instead, and remind myself how glorious nature is and how honored I am to be out in it.

I still struggle with finding clothing that fits, because I don't remember what size I am (it's different for every company). I utilize my Amazon Prime account so I can return things that don't fit and I do not get fixated on the numbers. I wear clothing that is comfortable, not child-sized, and I no longer attach myself to the size in my jeans.

I allow my body to change throughout a month, I am a woman and my body changes over the weeks. When I feel bloated and 'gross', I give myself permission to feel bloated and gross. I also acknowledge that it is because I am a woman and my body changes in time with my menstrual cycles. A valuable lesson for me over the past few years is knowing that my body has slight fluctuations in size, but if I am eating when I'm hungry and stopping when I am full, I stay pretty much the same size. It took years to realize this. My therapists continually told me this in my early stages of recovery, but I didn't fully understand the concept of not manipulating my body size until Advanced Recovery.

In the summer of 2021, I began working for a landscaping company which is, "back-breaking work…" I spent the summer wheeling heavy wheel-barrows, picking up rocks, cutting down trees, putting plants in the Earth, getting filthy everyday, and I didn't realize that my body changed and became the strongest, most beautiful body I could have ever imagined myself having. The beautiful part for me to experience was that I didn't care that I was bigger, bulkier, or any other adjective. I felt powerful. I felt strong. I felt capable. I left the job sites everyday knowing that I had used my strong body in ways I had never experienced. I loved my body for the first time ever. It was a glorious feeling that I will carry with me, close to my heart. In a spot where the eating disorder used to live.

It has taken me almost 10 years to circle back, surmise and finish this work. Everytime I think I am done experiencing triggers or learning more about myself and my eating disorder, another life experience comes along and challenges me once again. While I want to wait to publish it until I have it all figured out, I know that I never will have it figured out and it is time to share my experience and how I handle triggers now.

While wrapping up the writing of this book, I endured the most traumatic experiences of my life, back to back. In the midst of the COVID crisis, my father was diagnosed and then quickly passed of lung cancer. Two months later, the man I was planning on spending my life with left me, completely out of the blue- crushing me once again and shattering my trust in myself and my existence.

This book is not about my grief process regarding either of these experiences, it is about my healing, my ability to set boundaries, and most importantly how my eating disorder reacted to the stress.

The stress and anxiety that paralyzed me for weeks after both of these experiences caused me to lose my appetite. I was aware immediately that this could cause problems in my state of vulnerability. I recognised within a day or two after my father passed that I was not eating unless the meal was prepared, and plated, for me. I was not taking initiative to nourish myself. The most important thing I did in these days of crisis was to ask for help. I reached out to friends, specifically asking for them to cook meals and bring them to me. I shamelessly asked for help. I ate these meals prepared by my friends and family and I kept myself nourished so my brain had enough nutrients to process all of the grief and anxiety in the weeks following my father's death.

Following my breakup, my anxiety reached a level I had not experienced until that point. I tried, but I didn't get much sleep for almost three weeks. I was nauseous and threw up due to anxiety- not bulimia. And, again, I asked for help. I immediately contacted my grief counselor, who was helping me with my father's passing. She suggested another layer of support, so found a therapist. I contacted my dietician from CHS, even though I wasn't struggling with my eating disorder. I made the contact to add another layer of accountability and support. I texted, called, and visited friends I hadn't spoken with in awhile. I reached out and relied on my support system.

I contacted friends who I respect for their grace in handling challenging situations. I opened up to the strong women in my life and asked how they handled specific situations. I asked for help from my support system. I allowed my sister to cook for me every night. I allowed my friends to help me organize and go through my things and keep me on the path to healing. I reached out and found myself supported by a web of love that I had never allowed myself to feel before. I allowed myself to be hurt and vulnerable and weak, as I trusted a support system I never knew existed to this extent. I let myself hurt, I cried for weeks. I cried so hard my eyes swelled shut. I journaled about everything. Every single thought I had, I wrote it down. I read books and listened to podcasts about breakups, betrayal, self-worth.

I was depressed and paralyzed with anxiety, but I let my friends and family take care of me. I trusted them when they said, "eat", I'd eat. When they told me to sleep, I would try.

During these two traumatic events, my weight rocketed around. After my father passed, I didn't want to get out of bed for a few weeks and I didn't have the energy to maintain my active lifestyle. Whether I actually did or not, I felt like I gained weight. I referred to it as Bereavement Body. I wasn't worried about it, I didn't stress out about it, I accepted that it just was my body for now and I freed my brain to grieve.

After my breakup, I did lose weight. A lot of weight. I was not proud of it, and I kept having to reassure my support system that I wasn't engaging in eating disorder behaviors, that it was truly just nausea and anxiety that had limited my appetite. I wasn't proud or excited about this weight loss, but I was nervous about regaining it back. I know that when I am taking care of myself, my body levels out at a weight a bit higher than I was. I know how addicted I get to weight loss, so I remained hyper-aware of how I was reacting to this. I knew that I had my dietician and my therapist among other layers of support and I refused to let myself entertain the idea of engaging in eating disordered behaviors again.

I am very proud of how I've handled these experiences. I set boundaries for myself, knowing who I want to spend my time around and who drains me. When I started coming out of the initial acute grief my hunger returned, and I acknowledged it. I honored it. Because of these episodes of nausea and lack of appetite, I am even more in tune with my hunger signals and my fullness levels. This has caused me to dive deeper into listening to and acknowledging my needs. I hear my needs now immediately, whether it's regarding time alone, needing to see and spend time with certain people, avoid people, avoid activities or engage in activities. I feel and honor these needs immediately.

I am once again beyond grateful that I developed a healthy relationship with exercise, playtime. My playtime outdoors, in nature has healed me more than anything. If I was still wrapped up in calories and weight loss, my playtime out in nature would not have the healing effect that it did for me.

I FORGIVE MYSELF FOR ALL OF THE HURT
I HAVE INFLICTED ON MYSELF

Closing thoughts on recovery

I have gone on a lot of dates in the last few years. I have sat across countless tables from a partner, enjoying company immensely. It's hard to believe that this wasn't always the case. Hard to believe there was a time when I could hardly read menus through anxiety, that I couldn't pick up a utensil in a restaurant for fear of people watching me, that I couldn't enjoy company because the voices in my head were deafening. Hard to believe something that now brings me so much joy, once paralyzed me with fear. That seems like a lifetime ago. It seems almost silly now that the notion of wanting to date is what kept me motivated. But it was so real at the time. I wanted it badly enough that it helped define my recovery process.

Define your own recovery and what it looks like for you. Set your goals, even if they seem impossible. You don't even have to believe it's possible for you. I have lived it and I know it is possible, so I will believe for you. Trust yourself.

While in my recovery, a part of me believed that I was doomed. I was cursed with eating disordered thoughts. And, while these thoughts no longer ruled me (not even close) they are still there. They've dissipated to the point where, every few months, I'll have a disordered thought and it is a big indication that I need to address something in my life- whether it's relationship issues, general stress, or self-esteem issues. My eating disordered thoughts are indicative of something bigger and I need to pay attention.

I am constantly striving to appreciate my body in new ways, and I have accepted that there are days when I am not comfortable in my body. I know these days are temporary, I know they will pass.

I know my eating disorder would have scoured the pages of this book for tips and tricks, desperate to be triggered. However, I hope you were able to read it from a recovery minded point of view and dealt with these triggers as they surfaced. I know my eating disorder would have shamed me for wanting to leave such a friend behind.

If you are struggling with an eating disorder, put your armor on. Recovery is a battle, but go in knowing that you can, and will, win. I encourage you to turn your eating disorder inside-out. Figure out it's roots, what it means to you, it's importance in your life, dissect if fully. And most importantly begin to disentangle your own voice from that of the eating disorder. If you love your eating disorder because it is your best friend, because it is the only thing that belongs to you, it is the only thing that understands you, search your soul and begin to find your worth in other avenues. Place your energy and emphasis in finding people and activities who bring out the uniqueness in you and love you-focus on those connections. Start small: your smile, the way you park your car, the way you carry yourself at work, your taste in music. Own these beautiful aspects of your being.

Fight the urges. I promise you, they will fade in time. The more time that passes between each behavior, the easier it is to fight next time. The urges get weaker every time they surface when you do not engage in the behaviors. Do not fall for the voice in your head that says, "Just this last time, this will be the last time." No more last times. Do not engage in the behaviors. The urges will fade. Trust me.

Be authentic. Risk going into the world as the new you- the you without an eating disorder. The world will respond in your favor, they will love you, I promise. Speak your mind, speak your truths, be honest with yourself.

Find your playtime, healthily. Take care of your body, listen to its needs. Eat when you are hungry, stop when you are full, drink when you are thirsty, sleep when you are tired, cry when you are sad, scream when you are angry. Keep your living space clean and maintain the friendships that are important to you. This is all the stuff of real life, a life free from an eating disorder.

> Binge on love.
> Binge on laughter.
> Binge on challenges and self-awareness.
> Binge on real life.
> Be free.